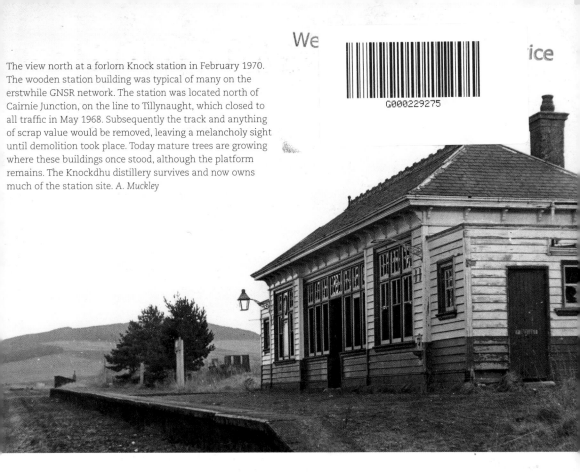

G000229275

The view north at a forlorn Knock station in February 1970. The wooden station building was typical of many on the erstwhile GNSR network. The station was located north of Cairnie Junction, on the line to Tillynaught, which closed to all traffic in May 1968. Subsequently the track and anything of scrap value would be removed, leaving a melancholy sight until demolition took place. Today mature trees are growing where these buildings once stood, although the platform remains. The Knockdhu distillery survives and now owns much of the station site. *A. Muckley*

Introduction

At their zenith the railways of Scotland provided a magnificent network, serving the needs of industrial and rural areas. The process of railway closures began to quicken after World War 2. Yet it was Dr Beeching's infamous 'Reshaping' report in the early 1960s which really accelerated the closure of lines and which, had it been fully implemented, would have left even larger areas of Scotland without any rail services.

As a result of all the closures Scotland has a remarkable heritage of disused railways and stations. Lost lines in Scotland are to be found in hugely dramatic and remote countryside. In contrast, many others are to be discovered in the midst of highly industrialised locations, providing an unparalleled diversity of lost lines and locations. Consequently, throughout Scotland a host of fascinating railway remains are still to be found.

Such are the losses in Scotland that this book adds to the first volume, *Lost Lines: Scotland*, focusing almost entirely on different lost lines and not duplicating any of the illustrations or text of the companion volume. Between them, the two free-standing books include more than 70 lost lines and give a flavour of the individuality of closed railways throughout Scotland.

Scotland has been at the forefront in rectifying the mistakes of the Beeching report. Railways once again serve Alloa and provide links to Bathgate, while reopening the northern section of the erstwhile Waverley route is under way.

Magnificence and melancholy

Scotland once had a wonderful network of railways. They developed a confident and distinctive look, becoming an integral part of Scottish communities. They conquered the rugged terrain and crossed huge expanses of water, but they never despoiled the beautiful countryside. While the northern latitude and physical height of several lines led to winter problems, particularly with snow, railways were to be found in some of the highest and remotest parts.

The original ex-HR main line, closed in October 1965, reached 1,052ft (321m) at Dava. The Wanlockhead branch in the Southern Uplands, which closed in January 1939, climbed to 1,498ft (456m) above sea level, making this the highest conventional passenger line in Britain.

The original ex-HR main line, closed in October 1965, reached 1,052ft (321m) at Dava. The Wanlockhead branch in the Southern Uplands,

which closed in January 1939, climbed to 1,498ft (456m) above sea level, making this the highest conventional passenger line in Britain.

The magnificence and beauty of Scotland were recognised in Victorian times. The railway companies actively encouraged tourism by naming trains, advertising scenic journeys and building hotels – often with golf courses. The railway-run hotels at Gleneagles, Turnberry and at Edinburgh were amongst the most luxurious and well known in Britain. On a smaller scale the HR provided hotels at Inverness, Kyle of Lochalsh, Strathpeffer and Dornoch. Whilst the GNSR hotel at Cruden Bay closed, the attraction of Scotland for tourists has remained strong, and all the other former railway hotels remain open, albeit none now in railway ownership.

Equally, Scotland is a country of contrasts, and, in sharp disparity to areas of great scenic beauty, areas of heavy industry and despoiled landscapes developed. Coal was once carried in huge quantities by the railways, particularly in the central lowlands, where coalfields such as those in Ayrshire, Lanarkshire, Fife and Midlothian all spawned an industrial network of railways. The great locomotive- and ship-building industries that developed in and around the Glasgow

Facing page Fraserburgh station on 15 June 1956, with BR Standard Class 4 2-6-4T No 80028 at the platform with the 11.28am Aberdeen train. The station had been enlarged and rebuilt in 1903. The Buchan lines north of Aberdeen once constituted an important system serving the sizeable towns of Peterhead and Fraserburgh. The busy freight yard will be noted, fish being the main source of traffic. *J. Halliday*

Below Fraserburgh passenger station and locomotive shed, the latter a sub-shed of Kittybrewster (61A), deserted and abandoned in February 1972. Freight would survive longer, until October 1979. The remaining track was lifted in 1980, and the derelict station buildings were demolished, but the stone-built locomotive shed still survives. *A. Muckley*

area were all once rail-served. Fish and minerals were also conveyed by rail, and freight-only lines could once be found even in remote parts of the Highlands and on some Scottish islands.

Yet all this was to change; parts of the railway network in Scotland were built in the optimistic boom years of the 19th century, and some lines serving isolated areas were based on unrealistic returns. In addition, after World War 1 road transport was already gaining momentum. The Grouping of 1923 saw the existing Scottish railway companies shared between the LNER and the LMS. This led to some rationalisation, and, coupled with an economic downturn, the 1920s and '30s saw a sprinkling of closures, but overall the Scottish network remained largely intact.

More significant decline came after World War 2, which had exhausted the railways, and, in a poor state of repair, they were nationalised in 1948. A distinct Scottish Region was created under the new British Railways, but such was the increasing drift toward road transport that the new region only ever made a profit in 1948 and 1951. A number of economies and rationalisations were implemented, and diesels introduced, but several lightly used secondary lines and branches lost their passenger services, although many lines were still retained for freight.

BR's losses continued to mount, and in 1963 massive cuts were proposed in the infamous Beeching report. This proposed that more than

50 passenger services be withdrawn in Scotland, identifying 425 stations and halts for closure and envisaging the complete annihilation of lines north and west of Inverness. Whilst political resistance led to some reprieves, the cuts resulted in the loss of lines from vast swathes of the country, the Borders, Galloway and Buchan being particularly badly hit.

Because of the sparse population of much of rural Scotland, some wayside stations always had very limited services. In 1960 all intermediate stations between Inverness and Tain were closed, with the exception of Dingwall, Invergordon and Fearn. This was just a foretaste of what was to come in the Beeching report. Even if a line was to be kept open, stopping services would often be discontinued and wayside stations closed; the Aberdeen–Inverness line, for example, has more than 30 closed intermediate stations.

Sadly even lines that were not proposed for closure in the Beeching report somehow lost their trains. St Andrews, Alloa and the main line to Perth via Kinross, all clearly retained in the report, saw their services withdrawn. Scotland's hitherto proud and extensive railway network was savagely cut; the mass closure of lines and stations continued in the name of making the railways more profitable, and

for many years the disused and mouldering remains of once well-maintained – indeed, in many cases impeccably maintained – stations and lines provided a melancholy sight.

The late 1960s saw the social obligations of the railway being acknowledged, and the fuel crisis of the early 1970s provided the realisation that without railways the country could be brought to a virtual standstill and further significant passenger closures were halted. Since then there have been many new or reopened stations on existing lines, while pro-rail policies and an active preservation movement have seen a number of lines restored to the Scottish network.

Left Lossiemouth station on 31 March 1964, with a DMU awaiting departure for Elgin. The line continued beyond the station to serve the harbour, and the conveniently sited Steamboat & Railway Hotel (left) was once used for meetings by the Lossiemouth Harbour Co. *W. Sumner*

Middle The view south at Lossiemouth, minus track, in June 1969, three years after closure of the line (in March 1966). The station buildings and Italianate Steamboat & Railway Hotel, seen on the left, would be demolished in 1988. The area is now a car park, and only a platform edge survives. *A. Muckley*

Left Tillynaught was the remote junction where the Banff line diverged from the Moray Coast line. The station is seen here with ex-CR 0-4-4T No 55185 on a Banff-branch train, comprising one ex-LNER coach and one ex-LMS, on 21 June 1958. *J. Halliday*

Left below Tillynaught station, closed in May 1968 and viewed here in the direction of Buckie, in February 1970. The station was just one of many to be closed at this time on the erstwhile GNSR, which suffered rather more than its fair share of closures. The derelict buildings were all subsequently demolished, and today there is little sign of the railway at this location. *A. Muckley*

Below St Andrews station on 6 July 1963, with Class B1 4-6-0 No 61099 having arrived with the 11.10am from Glasgow. On the left is the 1.58pm DMU to Dundee. The busy station, which was not identified for closure in the Beeching report, was well used and well connected to key destinations in Scotland. *W. Sumner*

Above Remnants of St Andrews station in September 2010. This photograph was taken just below where the lattice footbridge was once sited. The station has been demolished, and the section here has been filled in, but other parts survive in use as a car park. *Author*

Left BR map of Scotland in 1948, when much of the network remained in use.

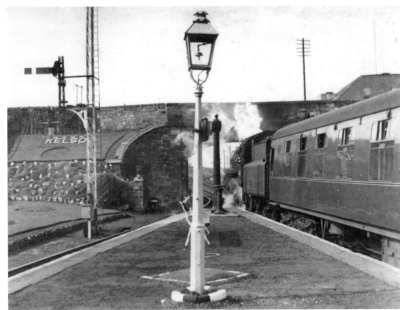

Above BR Standard Class 4 2-6-0 No 76050 at Kelso, the principal station on the Tweed Valley branch, with the morning through Berwick–St Boswells train on 11 April 1964. During World War 2 the line was busy with troops, including the author's father, who were stationed at Kelso prior to deployment in the war. *M. Dunnett*

Left Kelso station viewed in the direction of Coldstream, on 26 January 1974. After final closure, in April 1968, a period of dereliction followed before the once immaculately kept station and its gardens were demolished and swept away. Today Station Road is the only reminder of this once-important station. *A. Muckley*

Right Even main lines were closed. This is Riddings Junction, on the Waverley route, with Class J39 0-6-0 No 64727 at the Langholm platform, in June 1956. The branch to Langholm was one of the last of the short Waverley branches to close – to passengers in June 1964 and to freight in September 1967. The Waverley route itself closed in January 1969. *Ian Allan Library*

Left The view north at Riddings Junction on 19 February 1983. The buildings were gradually removed, and today the site is overgrown. Riddings Junction was located in England, but just south of the junction the line entered Scotland again for a short section; thus a Langholm–Carlisle train would cross the border three times during the course of its journey. *A. Muckley*

Below left The vast trainshed of Glasgow St Enoch station on 14 April 1966. The 5.30pm departures to East Kilbride and to Kilmarnock, via Barrhead, and the 5.33pm departure to Kilmarnock, via Dalry, are to be seen headed by 'Black Fives'. This magnificent station, celebrated as the Scottish equivalent of St Pancras, closed a couple of months later and was subsequently demolished. *L. Dopson*

Below right Although Glasgow St Enoch station was demolished, a hint of its grandeur remains in the attractive red-sandstone Jacobean-style St Enoch subway station. A new subway entrance has rendered this building surplus, and when this view was recorded, in September 2010, it was in use as a café. *Author*

Left Edinburgh Princes Street station in the spring of 1938, with a new streamlined LMS 'Coronation' Pacific working an evening train to Glasgow Central. *Charles Macpherson*

Below Towards the end of its life Princes Street took on a deserted air as remaining services were transferred to Waverley. The 'Caley' station, as it was known, is seen here in September 1965, just a few days before closure. It was subsequently demolished, but the adjoining former railway-owned Caledonian Hotel survives. *Author*

Above Class J36 0-6-0 No 65243 *Maude* (nowadays preserved) climbing from South Queensferry to Dalmeny with the morning freight in June 1963. Passenger services were withdrawn in January 1929, but the branch, which provided one of the last steam workings in Scotland, closed to all remaining traffic in November 1967. *The Rev R. Hughes*

Right The same bridge in September 2010. The Queensferry branch was close to the Firth of Forth, and a much broader arch carried the line under the Forth Bridge itself. The railway, in common with so many that have closed, has been turned into a delightful walkway. *Author*

2

The afterlife of arches

Scotland has many areas of rugged terrain and jagged coastline; there are many rivers, vast rolling hills and mountains, with the highest land in the British Isles. Scottish railways overcame this difficult terrain, for the most part, by climbing over high land and using valleys where possible. The result was fewer tunnels but more bridges and viaducts.

There is only one tunnel in Scotland of more than a mile in length, and the GNSR had only four tunnels in total. As a consequence some enormous viaducts were built, even on relatively insignificant branch lines, and, because much of the landscape is sparse and bleak, man-made structures can look particularly impressive. In fact the viaducts represent one of the most spectacular achievements of the railways in Scotland. They are found in an endless variety of designs and materials, but often using the local stone.

When a line closed, station buildings and land could be sold off relatively easily, but viaducts were another matter. Iron and steel structures could be dismantled and sold for scrap, while the safety issues arising from their deteriorating condition resulted in others being demolished, sometimes by being blown up. Yet the cost of demolishing some of these huge structures, which were solidly built in stone, brick or concrete, resulted in their survival.

Facing page Some of the 19 semicircular brick arches and elegant tapering stone piers of the ex-NBR Leaderfoot (also known as Drygrange) Viaduct, photographed on 9 August 1961. The train is an RCTS special, headed by ex-NBR 'D34' 4-4-0 *Glen Douglas* (now preserved) and a 'J37' 0-6-0. After 100 years of use the line closed in July 1965, but fortunately the finely crafted viaduct is preserved as a listed structure and is now used as a walkway. *G. Morrison*

Above Tarras Water Viaduct, on the ex-NBR Langholm branch, with an Ivatt Class 4 2-6-0 crossing shortly before closure, in 1964. The 12-span stone viaduct was opened a century earlier. The metal ties seen here were added later and prevented spreading of the outer walls. Many years after closure the viaduct was declared unsafe. Nonetheless, in 1987 demolition using explosives proved so difficult that two attempts had to be made. *John Spencer Gilks*

Right Saughtree Viaduct, to the east of Saughtree station, was also known as Dawstonburn Viaduct. Although relatively small in comparison with some viaducts, the sturdy four-span structure towered above the nearby road bridge over Dawstonburn. It would eventually be demolished in 1968, a decade after closure of the line. *Ian Allan Library*

Iron viaducts have fared least well, as after closure they were seen as expensive to maintain and a valuable source of scrap. By way of example, both the mile-long Solway Viaduct, opened in 1869 and closed in 1921, and the 1,610ft (490m) viaduct and swing bridge over the Forth near Alloa, opened in 1887 and closed in 1968, were dismantled for scrap.

In contrast many stone, brick and concrete viaducts remain, particularly in the great undulations of the Border Region and crossing Scotland's many rivers. The stone-built Laigh Milton

Viaduct, the oldest viaduct in Scotland and disused since 1845, was saved from collapse in the 1990s by the local council. Even plain brick viaducts provide a powerful effect by the repetitive pattern of their arches and their sheer size. Some viaducts, such as that at Leaderfoot, were a mixture of brick and stone; all were individually designed.

In the later years of railway construction stonemasons were becoming ever scarcer, and concrete was increasingly used as pioneered by Sir Robert McAlpine – or 'Concrete Bob', as he became known. Most concrete viaducts were built in a traditional arched style. At Risping Cleuch, on the Wanlockhead branch, the concrete viaduct was faced with terracotta bricks to improve its looks. Over the years frost loosened the bricks, some of which eventually fell off, and this prompted the demolition of the entire viaduct, using explosives, in 1991. Many other concrete structures remain, such as those on the Fort Augustus and St Fillans branches, as demolition is difficult and unlike metal structures, they have little or no scrap value.

Fortunately the destructive attitudes of the 1960s and '70s are for the most part a thing of the past, and the attractive design and quality of build of many viaducts is such that they have been 'listed' as being of architectural merit and have been saved for the nation. Historic Scotland is responsible for

Above A Leslie-branch goods train, originating from Markinch and headed by ex-LNER Class J38 0-6-0 No 65911, crosses the Balbirnie Viaduct over the River Leven on 12 September 1966, a year before closure. The 10-arch viaduct, built of local stone, dates from 1860 and was designed by Thomas Bouch; following the Tay Bridge disaster heavy cast-iron supports were added to most of its arches. It remains in use today as part of a cycle route. *J. French*

Below The ex-CR eight-arch Neidpath Viaduct was built in sandstone on a graceful curve over the River Tweed on the Peebles–Symington line. The masterpiece of skew-arch engineering, dating from 1864, fits well into the landscape and has survived since closure of the line in 1954, being used today as a footpath. This view was recorded in March 1993. *Author*

Above The 11-arch North Water Viaduct, built in 1865. The stone structure has five slightly skewed arches over the River North Esk in addition to six narrower arches – five at the north end and one at the south. The ex-NBR Bervie branch closed to all remaining traffic in May 1966, but in recent years the viaduct has reopened as part of a cycle path, this view being recorded in June 2009. *Author*

Above Big Water of Fleet Viaduct, on the Portpatrick & Wigtownshire Joint Railway, opened in 1861. The original stone structure began to subside and cracks appeared in the 1920s. Huge brick supports were required to strengthen the 20-arch structure, which nevertheless survived closure of the railway in June 1965, being seen here in July 2009. *Author*

many of the most important examples. Elsewhere heritage trusts, charities and local councils have stepped in with the aim of making disused viaducts accessible to the public as walkways or as part of a network of cycleways.

For many years those viaducts that had fallen into disuse were maintained by the BR Board Residuary Ltd, which examined each structure annually and carried out any essential repairs that were necessary to keep them in a safe condition. Fortunately most now have just the weight of a bicycle to support rather than a heavy freight train. Others, such as Connel Bridge on the Ballachulish branch, were converted entirely to road use and transferred to the appropriate highway authority.

Scotland is well known for its railway bridges, and fortunately the two most famous examples, the Forth Bridge (arguably the greatest railway bridge in the world) and the second Tay Bridge (the longest in Britain) continue to be used by trains. These bridges, together with many others that remain extant but are disused, now occupy a place deep in the heart of Scotland.

15

Above The swing bridge over the River Forth at Alloa was built to carry the CR's line south of the town and was opened in 1885. The half-mile-long structure was known as 'the other Forth Rail Bridge' and was last used in 1968. The fixed wrought-iron lattice-girder spans and swing sections were dismantled in 1971 to be sold for scrap, but most of the stone piers and their riveted iron ties remain. *Ian Allan Library*

Left Connel Bridge, on the Ballachulish branch, with ex-CR 0-4-4T No 55263 crossing in August 1959. The steel cantilever bridge with a single span of 500ft (152m) was required because of the rapid tidal flow at this point. It was opened in 1903, and in 1913 tolls were introduced for use of the road (right) across the bridge, although road traffic was halted when a train was crossing. The trains ceased running in 1966, but the impressive structure remains in use as a road bridge. *P. Ransome-Wallis*

Below A DMU on the Lanark–Muirkirk line crosses over the River Clyde by means of Sandilands Viaduct, south of Lanark, on 22 May 1964. Designed by George Graham, the viaduct was completed in 1861. The six-span bowstring-girder section would be dismantled and sold for scrap following closure of the railway in 1968, but the huge stone buttresses, particularly evident at the southern end of the viaduct, remain. *John Spencer Gilks*

Above Speymouth Viaduct, at Garmouth, was built by Blaikie Bros and opened in 1886. The bowed central truss measured some 350ft (106m) from end to end, while six 100ft (30m) approach spans were also provided. The viaduct was so designed because of the wandering nature of the fast-flowing Spey; indeed the river has changed course and currently flows under one of the 100ft spans rather than the main central one. Despite years of disuse following closure of the Moray Coast line (in 1968) it escaped demolition and is now used as a footpath. *D. Walters*

Above The Loch Ken Viaduct, near Parton, consists of three main bowstring-girder spans – each 138ft (42m) long – over Loch Ken itself and two stone arches on each approach. Dating from 1861, it was saved following closure of the Dumfries–Stranraer 'Port Road' in 1965 and is now used by a private farm track; this photograph was taken in July 2009. *Author's collection*

Left The curved concrete viaduct spanning the Ogle Burn at Lochearnhead. There are seven 40ft (12m) spans and two half-spans at each end. The design includes 'channelling' and headstone effects moulded into the concrete. The viaduct dates from 1904, although the effect of weathering has been such that parts look like new, while others are stained black. Although some water seepage is apparent, the drainage was still working well when this photograph was taken on a wet day in October 2011. *Author's collection*

3

Border branches

This chapter looks at the network of branches that fed into the ex-NBR Waverley route from Edinburgh to Carlisle. Because of the undulating nature of the Borders some were expensive to construct, but agricultural traffic was once extensive. The Cheviot sheep provided steady revenue; their wool was used by the Border mill towns, which in turn mostly required coal, while even the tweed from the area was once conveyed by rail.

By comparison passenger traffic was quite light. In September 1932 the Lauder branch lost its passenger services, and in April the following year the Gifford branch. As road transport assumed greater influence several other branches became candidates for closure, particularly after BR took control. Equally, some lines in the Borders met premature ends, due to damage caused by severe flooding in August 1948.

In essence the Border lines fell into two categories: the short branches connecting more important settlements to the main line, and longer meandering secondary links that were sometimes opened in stages. Today all are lost.

The Peebles Railway opened in July 1855 and encouraged commuters to relocate from Edinburgh to fine houses within easy reach of Peebles station. The huge Peebles Hydro Hotel promoted tourist

Facing page Hardengreen Junction, one of many junctions on the Waverley route, on 17 August 1963, with the 3.35pm Millerhill–Carlisle freight, headed by 'Black Five' 4-6-0 No 44886, passing the former Peebles branch in the foreground. By this time the remaining freight-only line had been cut back to the Penicuik branch, the final section of this line, to Eskbank Paper Mill, closing in 1967. *R. Montgomery*

Right The ex-NBR yard at Peebles pictured in the snow in November 1961, with Peebles Junction box on the right and the connection to the ex-CR Peebles West station over to the left. Little activity is apparent, and all the lines seen here were to close three months later. *D. Smith*

use of the line, and the 'Peebles-shire Express' ran from Edinburgh. The railway was taken over by the NBR in 1876. Its decline was a long-drawn-out affair, and the 45½-mile line from Edinburgh to Galashiels via Peebles, which on weekdays latterly saw just three trains in each direction, finally closed to all traffic in February 1962.

The Caledonian Railway's 19-mile branch from Peebles West to Symington was opened throughout by February 1864. Although connection was made with the NBR at Peebles this was little used, and the line became a rural backwater. At one time the branch was noted for its meat trains dispatched to London, but gradually agricultural and passenger traffic drifted onto the roads. Closure to passengers came in June 1950, with little protest, and to through freight four years later.

The 6½-mile branch to Selkirk opened in April 1856 and provided through services to Galashiels, which did much to revive Selkirk. An additional intermediate station at Abbotsford opened in 1900

but closed in 1931, except for Braw Lads Gathering passenger specials. The branch closed to passenger traffic in September 1951, and to remaining freight in November 1964.

The 30¾-mile Reston–St Boswells line was a westerly extension of the Reston–Duns branch, which had opened in August 1849. Completion of the huge Leaderfoot Viaduct permitted the opening of the entire route in October 1865. Although built for double track and to main-line standards, it was opened as a single track save for the Reston–Duns section, and even this was soon singled. The NBR line never met expectations and remained a secondary route. The Duns–Greenlaw section closed following flood damage in August 1948. Reston–Duns passenger services were restored but were barely viable and were withdrawn in September 1951. In July 1965 the Ravenswood Junction–Greenlaw freight section closed, that between Reston and Duns following in November 1966.

The 11½-mile NBR St Boswells–Kelso line opened in June 1851 and was extended to connect

ST BOSWELLS

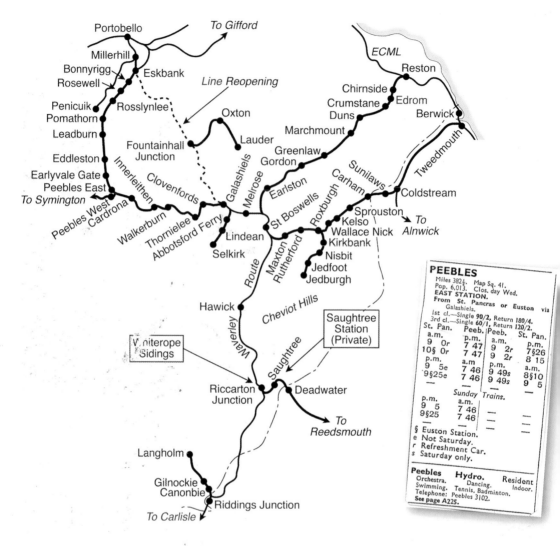

PEEBLES
Miles 382¼. Map Sq. 41.
Pop. 6,013. Clos. day Wed.
EAST STATION.
From St. Pancras or Euston via
Galashiels.
1st cl.—Single 90/2, Return 180/4.
3rd cl.—Single 60/1, Return 120/2.

St. Pan.	Peeb.	Peeb.	St. Pan.
a.m.	p.m.	a.m.	p.m.
9 Or	7 47	9 2r	7§26
10§ Or	7 47	9 2r	8 15
p.m.	a.m	p.m.	a.m.
9 5e	7 46	9 49s	8§10
9§25e	7 46	9 49s	9 5
—	—	—	—

Sunday Trains.

p.m.	a.m.		
9 5	7 46	—	—
9§25	7 46	—	—
—	—		

§ Euston Station.
e Not Saturday.
r Refreshment Car.
s Saturday only.

Peebles   Hydro.   Resident
Orchestra.   Dancing.   Indoor.
Swimming. Tennis, Badminton.
Telephone: Peebles 3102.
See page A225.

with the NER east of Kelso. This provided a link to Tweedmouth, some 22¼ miles distant, creating a through route between St Boswells and Berwick. The line provided the NER with its only two stations north of the border. For a time some passenger trains ran from Edinburgh to Berwick via Galashiels and Kelso, and for three months in 1948, due to flooding on the East Coast main line, Anglo-Scottish workings were diverted via this route. The St Boswells–Tweedmouth passenger service was withdrawn in June 1964. Kelso–Tweedmouth freight traffic ceased in March 1965, and the remaining St Boswells–Kelso freight followed suit in April 1968.

The 7-mile Jedburgh branch opened in July 1856. The station was some way from the town, but agricultural traffic was extensive. At Kirkbank, a small intermediate station, almost 12,000 head of livestock were dispatched during 1920, which was a peak time for the railways in the area. Passenger services on the branch came to a sudden end when it was severed by floods in August 1948. Repairs were undertaken allowing freight to continue, but the line closed to this traffic in August 1964.

The Riccarton Junction–Reedsmouth line formed part of a 42-mile secondary route to Hexham. The line opened as a through route at

Facing page below Peebles ABC Guide 1956

Top right The exterior of Selkirk railway station in 1950. The branch to the town was completed by April 1856, and woollen mills once employed more than 1,000 workers making woollen tweeds and tartans. Passenger services ceased in September 1951, and final closure came in November 1964. The stone-built station was demolished in the 1970s. *Real Photos*

Below right Duns station following the traditional cattle fair, on 18 September 1950. On the left can be seen a typical ex-NBR signalbox, but by 1963 the box had been demolished, and the line through the station singled. Following final closure, in November 1966, the main station building survived as part of an engineering firm's reuse of the site. *H. Bowtell*

the same time as the Waverley route, in July 1862. From Reedsmouth a 25-mile link continued to Morpeth, and from Scotsgap a branch ran to Rothbury. While all part of the NBR, the lines were mainlyin Northumberland and are thus covered in greater detail in *Lost Lines: North Eastern*.

Langholm, one of the larger settlements not on the Waverley route, was served by a 7-mile branch from Riddings Junction, opened in April 1864. Through trains ran to Carlisle, but the line closed to passenger traffic in June 1964 and to all traffic in September 1967. In January 1969 the Waverley route was itself closed, and BR quickly lifted the track at Riddings Junction, demonstrating its determination to kill the route.

Below Brush Type 4 No D1976 passes Selkirk Junction with the 14.45 Edinburgh–Carlisle service on 4 April 1966. A short section of the Selkirk branch still existed at this time to serve Netherdale siding but was destined to close in October 1966. *G. Kingmorn*

Above Greenlaw station on 29 May 1959, with Class J36 0-6-0 No 65233 having arrived with a pick-up goods. After closure of the Greenlaw–Duns section, due to flood damage in 1948, the station remained until July 1965 as the terminus of the freight-only line from Ravenswood Junction. The station house survives today as a private dwelling. *John Spencer Gilks*

Right Earlston station on the occasion of the last freight train, on 16 July 1965. The diesel-hauled train was destined for St Boswells. Passenger services had been withdrawn due to flooding in 1948 and were never restored. The former station is now part of an industrial area. *B. McMacartney*

Right Near Kelso Junction in July 1961, with ex-NBR Class J36 0-6-0 No 65330 heading the Tweedmouth–St Boswells pick-up goods, comprising an assortment of wagons. The telephone box at the base of the signal would be used by the crew if the train were held at the signal, and the signal itself doubled as a telephone pole. Goods traffic here ceased in August 1964. *J. Baker*

Right Roxburgh in July 1961, with ex-NBR Class D34 4-4-0 No 62484 *Glen Lyon* waiting to leave with a freight from the Jedburgh branch. Freight traffic survived until August 1964. The station building just visible on the far left of the picture remains extant today as a private dwelling. *D. Esau*

Left Branch superpower: 'Jubilee' 4-6-0 No 45696 *Arethusa* with a short freight train leaving Nisbet, one of three intermediate stations on the Jedburgh branch, on 29 May 1964. Nisbet station survives as a private residence, while a section of trackbed north of the station forms part of the Borders Abbey Way footpath. *John Spencer Gilks*

Right Jedfoot station was originally called Jedfoot Bridge. Here Ivatt 2-6-0 No 43138 awaits opening of the level-crossing gates outside the station with a freight train on 18 July 1963. Freight traffic survived until August 1964, but little now remains of the station. *John Spencer Gilks*

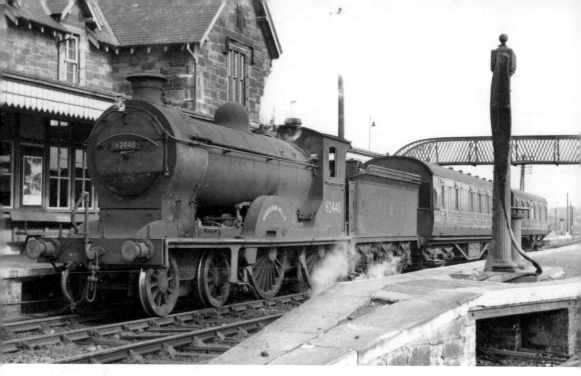

Above Kelso was the key station on the St Boswells–Berwick line. Here ex-NBR Class D30 4-4-0 No 62440 *Wandering Willie* calls with a St Boswells local train on 25 September 1954. In 1941 the LNER had produced posters extolling the beauty of Kelso, on the banks of the River Tweed. *Ian Allan Library*

Left Saughtree, the first stop beyond Riccarton Junction, on 28 April 1952. At this time the remote and lonely station was served by one train in each direction on three days a week only. The current owner has re-laid a short stretch of line here and runs a number of items of rolling stock. *H. C. Casserley*

Right The Langholm-branch terminus on 31 August 1962, with Ivatt Class 4 2-6-0 No 43045 ready to depart with the 3.30pm two-coach train to Carlisle. The station at one time had an overall roof. After closure in September 1967 the station was demolished, and the area seen here is now a car park. *Ian Allan Library*

Above Ivatt Class 4 2-6-0 No 43011 near Gilnockie with the Langholm-branch afternoon train to Carlisle on 6 April 1963. Gilnockie station had been added in November 1864, subsidence affecting one arch of the nearby Byreburn Viaduct having disrupted through services on the branch. The station house survives in private ownership. *W. Smith*

Right Class J39 0-6-0 No 64895 approaches Gilnockie on 8 August 1962 with the 9.10am from Langholm. This locomotive was used occasionally on the branch and was one of the last ex-LNER locomotives working from Carlisle Canal shed. All of this class had been withdrawn by the end of 1962. *S. Crook*

4

Killed in Kirkcudbright

The Castle Douglas–Kirkcudbright line opened to freight in February 1864. After a delay to rectify problems with the line speed and signal arrangements at the junction with the 'Port Road' at Castle Douglas the branch opened to through passengers in August 1864.

The 11-mile single-track line from Castle Douglas followed a scenic route, crossing the River Dee and meandering through sparsely populated countryside to reach Kirkcudbright. Here a handsome stone terminus was built, in keeping with the attractive county town located at the mouth of the River Dee.

Although built by the Kirkcudbright Railway, the branch was worked from the outset by the GSWR, which assumed full control in 1865. Even though the line was a branch off the 'Port Road' to Ireland, which westward from Castle Douglas was owned jointly by the CR, GSWR and MR, the principal passenger service to develop on the branch involved through trains to and from Dumfries, some 30 miles from Kirkcudbright, over what was at one time a section of line wholly owned by the GSWR.

Even though the branch served a remote area, livestock and other agricultural traffic was once quite substantial. The new line was well patronised and in turn provided new prosperity for Kirkcudbright. Tarff, one of two intermediate stations on the branch, even had pretensions to serve Gatehouse of Fleet, but in later years bus services ran from Kirkcudbright. There was fish traffic from the harbour, and oyster

Right Map of Kirkcudbright, 1900. *Crown copyright*

Facing page Dalbeattie station on 23 April 1965, with
a BR Standard Class 4 2-6-4T No 80117 on the 2.50pm
Dumfries–Kirkcudbright train, just a couple of weeks before
withdrawal of the service (on 5 May). On the platform are
three railway employees – but no passengers. *D. Smith*

ships once landed at Kirkcudbright, using the
railway to transport their catch to London, until the
beds were exhausted.

Kirkcudbright enjoyed a long association with
the Glasgow Art movement and became known
as the 'artists' town'. Charles Oppenheimer, one of
Kirkcudbright's more famous resident artists, was
commissioned by BR to create a poster of nearby
Kippford and the Solway coast, and for many years a
copy was proudly displayed at Kirkcudbright station.

Dorothy L. Sayers provided a description of
Kirkcudbright in her book *Five Red Herrings*, written in
1931; the plot involved murder committed within the
artistic community and included a train-ticket puzzle.
Little changed over the years on the Kirkcudbright
line, and no real attempt was made at modernisation.
In September 1946 the intermediate station at Bridge
of Dee closed to regular passengers. In 1963 a freight
train failed to stop at the terminus and pushed

a passenger coach, standing at the platform, across the
adjoining road – fortunately without loss of life.

Nonetheless the branch traffic gradually slipped
away as freight and passengers increasingly travelled
by road. The line's fate was sealed by its inclusion
on page 124 of the Beeching report; there was to be
no reprieve. Passenger and freight services ceased in
May and June 1965 respectively, resulting in the line's
closure after just over a century of use, decimating
the railways in this part of Scotland.

The main station building at Kirkcudbright
remains, as do the station buildings at Tarff and Bridge
of Dee. The box girder of the viaduct over the River
Dee has been removed, but the stone piers survive, and
numerous remnants of this heavily engineered line are
evident in the landscape.
The history of the Castle
Douglas–Stranraer line
is covered in *Lost Lines:
Joint Railways*.

Left Kirkcudbright–
Gatehouse of Fleet bus
services, summer 1950.

Right ABC Guide for April
1956.

KIRKCUDBRIGHT			
Miles 362¼. Map Sq. 43.			
Pop. 2,498. Clos. day Thur.			
From St. Pancras or Euston via			
Castle Douglas.			
1st cl.—Single 85/5, Return 170/10.			
3rd cl.—Single 56/11, Return 113/10.			
St. Pan.	Kirkc.	Kirkc.	St. Pan.
a.m.	p.m.	a.m.	a.m.
10 0r	6 58	8 30r	5§15
p.m.	a.m.	9 35r	7 20
9 15e	7 36	p.m.	
11§50e	9 10	12 22sr	9§ 0
			a.m.
—	4 51s		4§58
—	4 51e		5§ 5
	Sunday Trains.		
p.m.	a.m.		
9 15	7 36	—	—
11§40	9 10		
§ Euston Station.			
e Not Saturday.			
r Refreshment Car.			
s Saturday only.			
Buses from Dumfries, Whitesands,			
approx. every two hours (hourly on			
Saturday), 75 min. journey.			

Table 131 Gatehouse of Fleet and Kirkcudbright (Via Twynholm)										
Leave	am	am	a.m	p.m	pm	pm	pm	p.m		S0
Gatehouse of Fleet	8 49	4 10	4 12	42 44	4 6	9 8		4 10p5		
Kirkcudbright arr.	8 33	9 33	10 33	12 33	233	4 33	6 38	8 33	10 33	
	a.m	a.m.	a.m	p.m	p.m	pm	p.m	S0		
Kirkcudbright lev.	7 32	8 32	11 18	1 18	3 20	5 30	7 32	9p27		
Gatehouse ....arr.	8 1	9 1	11 46	1 46	3 48.5	5 58	8 1	9 56		

Above BR Standard Class 4 2-6-4T No 80023 passing Southwick station on 13 July 1963 with the 12.30pm Kirkcudbright–Dumfries service. Although the station appears almost derelict it was still advertised in the summer timetable; this train was scheduled to call but, in the absence of passengers, did not stop. *M. Mensing*

Middle No 80023 disturbs the rustic idyll (and semi-dereliction) at Tarff with the 3.30pm train from Castle Douglas to Kirkcudbright. Originally called 'Tarff for Gatehouse' and later 'Gatehouse', the station adopted its final title in 1871. It closed in June 1965, although the station house survives as a private residence. *E. Gadsden*

Left The 9.25am Kirkcudbright–Castle Douglas train arriving at Tarff behind BR Standard Class 4 2-6-0 No 76073 on 16 April 1965. An agricultural co-operative was established at the station in 1903 to supply tenant farmers in the area with coal, lime and other goods arriving at the station. The agricultural depot and station house remain extant today. *W. Sumner*

Left BR Standard Class 4 2-6-4T No 80023 crossing Tongland Viaduct over the River Dee on 11 July 1963 with the 9.30am Kirkcudbright–Castle Douglas train. The line closed in June 1965, and the central box-girder section of the viaduct was removed the following year, but the stone piers remain.
M. Mensing

Right Dignity ecclesiastical and mechanical. Ex-LMS Class 2P 4-4-0 No 40614 spends a quiet hour at Kirkcudbright before taking out the 4.54pm to Dumfries on 30 July 1952. The handsome terminus, in keeping with the town, is seen in the distance. The Midland influence is apparent in this view, and through coaches once ran to St Pancras.
Ian Allan Library

Below A mixed rake forming the 8am Dumfries train, headed by BR Standard Class 4 2-6-4T No 80117, at Kirkcudbright on 16 April 1965. The well-built stone terminus in St Mary Street survives in use as shops, but the rest of the former station site has been redeveloped as housing. *W. Sumner*

5

Thin Ayr

The county of Ayr is one of contrasts. While Glaswegians flocked by train to the beautiful Ayrshire coast, where sandy beaches were warmed by the Gulf Stream, elsewhere there were despoiled areas of coal extraction. Some opencast coal workings continue today, and in the hills of central Ayrshire coal trains still use a number of secondary lines that have long since been closed to passengers.

On the coast, Heads of Ayr station opened in 1906 as part of Maidens & Dunure Light Railway, which was built primarily to serve the GSWR's Turnberry Hotel. The line was an early casualty and closed to passengers in December 1930. It reopened in July 1932 for a couple of through trains to Turnberry (see *Lost Lines: Scotland*), but other intermediate stations were not reopened, and the line closed to passengers once more in June 1933.

The 3-mile Heads of Ayr–Alloway Junction section again reopened to passengers in May 1947, to serve a new Butlin's holiday camp located east of the Heads of Ayr. A new station with a single platform and utilitarian building was opened by the LMS, actually inside the holiday camp, which came into use at the same time. The campsite had been built by Butlin's during World War 2, on the orders of the Admiralty as a naval training camp, but with the plan for it to become a holiday camp when the war ended.

The holiday camp was a great success, and thousands of 'happy campers' used the site, particularly in the 1950s. For many the train was

Facing page With the impressive Heads of Ayr as a backdrop, Class B1 4-6-0 No 61219 is pictured shortly after leaving the Butlin's campsite station with the 1.35pm train for Ayr. The photograph is undated but would have been taken during the summer season in the early 1960s, and the locomotive and its eight coaches had arrived on a through working from Edinburgh. *D. Cross*

Right Approaching Heads of Ayr station with a train from Ayr on 14 September 1968. This was the penultimate train to use the branch and was hauled by English Electric Type 1 diesel No D8124. On the right of the picture can be seen the gantry that formed part of the Butlin's holiday camp's 1,560ft (475m) chair lift, which survived until 1998. *D. Cross*

Left The same train at the Heads of Ayr station. In addition to two standard-gauge static locomotives, the holiday camp also had a miniature railway. This had three locomotives and ran from 1956 to 1988, from the centre of the camp to the beach gate. The miniature railway and main-line station site are now lost under redevelopment and a number of caravan pitches. *D. Cross*

the only way to get to the relatively remote (but self-contained) facilities. Initially there was a single train on Saturdays, but this soon increased, with local services to and from Ayr and Kilmarnock and long-distance trains to and from destinations as far away as Newcastle and Leeds. Trains ran on summer Saturdays only, this being the day that camp holidays started or ended.

The original Heads of Ayr station remained open for goods, but the new station became a terminus in 1955 when the remainder of the erstwhile light railway closed to all traffic. Although Dr Beeching was keen to 'damp down' the rail-holiday traffic in the 1960s, the branch line was not proposed for closure in his report; instead the plan envisaged Heads of Ayr as a railhead, the main line south to Stranraer being listed for closure.

The holiday camp already boasted a chair lift and a miniature railway, but 1964 saw ex-LMS Pacific No 6233 *Duchess of Sutherland* (towed to the camp by rail) and ex-London, Brighton & South Coast Railway 'Terrier' 0-6-0T No 62 *Martello* added as new static attractions, train-spotting being then in full swing. Billy Butlin would later be recognised for his work in rescuing a number of fine locomotives for use as attractions at his camps.

The appeal of British holiday camps declined somewhat in the 1960s, and car ownership increased. The last train to Butlin's Heads of Ayr station ran on

16 September 1968, coinciding with the seasonal closure of the camp; subsequently holidaymakers would have no option but to travel by road. In 1971 the locomotives left the site by road for Bressingham Steam Museum and eventual restoration to working order. In 1988 the miniature railway closed, but the three miniature locomotives were all found new homes. Lamp-posts and some remnants of the main-line station could still be found in 2000, when the original camp was demolished to be replaced by a new structure. Today there is little evidence of any of the railways associated with the holiday camp, although much of the trackbed of the line to the camp is used as a cycleway.

Above Stanier Class 8F 2-8-0 No 48536 in charge of a weedkilling train, seen shortly after crossing the stone-built Doon Viaduct at Alloway in May 1961. The railway viaduct still survives at this location, just downriver from the famous 'Brig o' Doon'. *D. Cross*

Left The 9.45am Heads of Ayr–Glasgow St Enoch, headed by BR Standard Class 4 2-6-4T No 80051, in a sylvan setting near the site of the former Alloway station. Note the route semaphore on the locomotive smokebox. Like most of the stations on the former Maidens & Dunure Light Railway, Alloway station had essentially consisted of an island platform and a coal siding. *W. Hamilton*

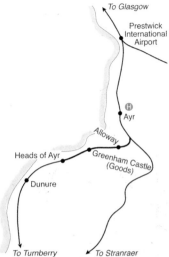

Above In charge of a Heads of Ayr–Leeds train in August 1958, BR Standard Class 5 4-6-0 No 73123 passes the site of the old Alloway station, easily identified by the widened section of cutting. Alloway is the birthplace of Robert Burns. *D. Cross*

Below Ex-LMS 'Crab' 2-6-0 No 42806 near Greenan Castle goods sidings, between the Heads of Ayr and Alloway, on 21 May 1963 with an Irvine–Heads of Ayr ballast train used for repacking the track and clearing scrub. *D. Cross*

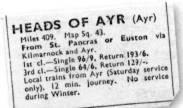

HEADS OF AYR (Ayr)
Miles 409. Map Sq. 43.
From St. Pancras or Euston via Kilmarnock and Ayr.
1st cl.—Single 96/9, Return 193/6.
3rd cl.—Single 64/6, Return 129/-.
Local trains from Ayr (Saturday service only), 12 min. journey. No service during Winter.

Above ABC Guide, April 1956.

Facing page Maryhill Central station on 2 September 1963, with Fairburn 2-6-4T No 42694 on a Rutherglen–Possil empty-stock train and sister locomotive No 42125 (right) departing with a train for Whifflet Upper. The station has been demolished since closure, and the site redeveloped, but a tunnel space has been provided under the new development in case of reopening, and the road bridges remain. *M. Finlay*

Above Preparing to surrender the single-line token on approaching Alloway Junction with a train for Ayr hauled by 'Crab' 2-6-0 No 42909 on 5 June 1965. The long train would be conveying passengers making a sad return home from their holidays. *D. Cross*

Above right Freight having ceased in 1959, the very last train from the Heads of Ayr – a DMU formation bound for Glasgow – is seen coming off the branch at Alloway Junction, on 14 September 1968. The site of the junction, on the Ayr–Stranraer line, is still identifiable today. *D. Cross*

Right The 429ft (130m) Alloway Tunnel, seen from the Doon Viaduct entrance in October 2011. The cut-and-cover tunnel was built to conceal the railway from the nearby ruined kirk, of Robert Burns fame, and consequently is also sometimes called the Auld Alloway Kirk Tunnel. Nowadays it forms part of a long-distance cycle route. *Author*

6

Ghosts of Glasgow's past

The first railway to reach Glasgow was the Garnkirk & Glasgow Railway, in 1831, conveying both goods and passengers. There followed a period of almost continuous railway development, and by 1900 the city could boast two steam-operated underground railways and a cable-operated subway.

The Glasgow tram network also grew and was electrified. The speedy 'caurs', as they became known, were both well loved and used. The development of frequent inner-suburban tram services spelled an end to a number of passenger services on suburban railway lines, that to Govan closing to passengers as early as 1902. The success of the electric trams also meant that the stations on the Paisley & Barrhead District Railway, at Ferguslie, Stanely, Glenfield, Barrhead New, Barrhead South, Dykebar and Paisley East, never opened for passenger traffic.

The Glasgow Central Railway was originally proposed as an overhead line, as in Liverpool, but after strong opposition it eventually became a costly 7-mile, mainly underground railway, serving the inner suburbs. Tunnelling under the city's busy streets was fraught with difficulties, and problems even arose in the West End, where an unobtrusive station had to be provided at Botanic Gardens. Running through central Glasgow from Maryhill to Newton, the line opened in stages during the period 1894-6 as part of the CR and in its early days was very busy. Third-class workmen's trains ran at peak times, and connections were made to other lines. Of prime importance was the Rutherglen–Maryhill service, but there were also through passenger services to Balloch and to Coatbridge, while numerous freight trains operated over the route.

Decline came over many years. At first fewer trains stopped at some intermediate stations; individual stations then closed, following which trains trundled past deserted platforms at Botanic Gardens (from February 1939), Kirklee (May 1939), Kelvin Bridge (August 1952) and Anderston (August 1959). Maryhill–Stobcross passenger services ceased in November 1959. In July 1964 almost all residual freight was taken off the line, and the remaining steam-operated passenger services, worked by dirty and run-down stock, were withdrawn in October of that year. The railway and many of its connections were simply abandoned. Later plans for a complete reopening with electric trains did not proceed, although the Bridgetown–Stobcross section was reopened in 1979.

The Lanarkshire & Dunbartonshire Railway opened from Dumbarton and hugged the industrialised north bank of the Clyde to reach Partick West in 1896. Within the city boundary the railway turned northeastward through Kelvinside, joining the Glasgow Central Railway to reach Maryhill and Possil. It became part of the extensive

Below The viaduct over the River Kelvin, southwest of Maryhill Central station, pictured in October 2011. Two viaducts crossed the river here, this being the structure erected by the Glasgow Central Railway. Of note is the telegraph pole that still survives on the viaduct. *Author*

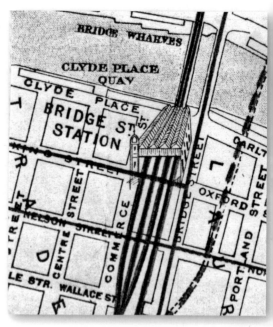

Above Diagrammatic map of Bridge Street station, south of Central station, *c*1900, with its overall roof; the nearby tram routes and subway line are also indicated. *Author's collection*

Below Botanic Gardens station was located between Botanic Tunnel to the north and Great Western Tunnel to the south. The subterranean platforms lie below Glasgow's Botanic Gardens. Light and ventilation was provided by this white-glazed-brick shaft, which ran the length of the platforms. In 1900 the station handled more than 100,000 passengers, but competition from trams became so intense that it was the first station on the line to be closed, in 1939. The platforms still exist and could be seen beneath these vents in October 2011. *Author*

Above The 1.30pm DMU train from Coatbridge Central arrives at Possil on 24 April 1963. Although acting as a terminus for most passenger services this was a through station, and the main station building spanned the through tracks. It closed in October 1964. *L. Sandler*

Below Bridgeton Cross station closed in October 1964 and is seen here in a derelict state in July 1972, this being the view towards Glasgow Green. The Rutherglen platforms reopened in November 1979, but the island platform for Carmyle (right) remains disused, although it could still be found under the road in 2012. *Ian Allan Library*

Bottom Just north of Kelvin Bridge station, where the platforms were located in part over the River Kelvin, the line ran into the 700yd (640m) tunnel under Great Western Road. Although plans to electrify the line were considered in 1898 they were never implemented. The tunnel was last used in 1964, and the southern portal is seen here in October 2001. *Author*

CR network in Glasgow in 1909 and eventually part of the LMS. The duplication of lines north of the River Clyde saw the Dumbarton–Rutherglen passenger service withdrawn in October 1964. The remaining freight traffic between Partick Central and Yoker Yard ceased in October 1978, although the Dalmuir–Clydebank section remained open for freight until June 1991.

In addition to the closure of the large St Enoch and Buchanan Street termini (outlined in detail in *Lost Lines: Scotland*) a number of intermediate stations on other surface lines that remained open in the Glasgow area have also been closed over the years. By way of example, south of the Clyde, Bridge Street closed in 1905, Gorbals in 1928, Bellahouston in 1954, Strathbungo in 1962, Cumberland Street in 1966 and Ibrox in 1967.

Given the number of closed stations (more than 50) in and around Glasgow, both on lines that have closed and on those that remain open, it is perhaps not surprising that a number of ghost stories have been reported – most notably in relation to the subway, where spectral forms and strange noises have been described in chilling detail. Although Glasgow still has the UK's largest suburban rail network outside London, the remnants of its closed stations provide a ghostly reminder of its lost lines

Above After closure the substantial brick-built Possil station on the road overbridge, inscribed with CR monograms, gradually became more derelict. The building survived in October 2011, as seen here, but was in a poor state of repair and considered to be 'at risk'. *Author*

Above Kelvinside station was opened by the CR in 1896. The sandstone building was built in an Italian Renaissance style and was adjacent to the southern portal of the 700yd (640m) Balgray Tunnel. The station closed to passengers in 1942, but, being a listed building, it still survives and is seen here in September 2009 in use as a restaurant. *Author*

Right Ex-CR 0-6-0 No 57607 crosses the River Kelvin after leaving Partick Central station with a Dalmuir–Rutherglen train on 5 August 1957. Partick Central station closed to all traffic in 1978, but the main station buildings escaped demolition until 2007. *G. Robin*

Left Headed by ex-CR 0-6-0 No 57554, a Rutherglen–Balloch Central train leaves Partick West on 2 August 1957 as a WD 'Austerity' 2-8-0 waits on the west side of the triangle with empties for the docks. After a period of dereliction following final closure much of the area has been redeveloped. *G. Robin*

Left A Metro-Cammell DMU departs Partick West as the 12.20pm Maryhill Central–Coatbridge on 30 September 1964. Partick West was the junction for the ex-Lanarkshire & Dunbartonshire Railway lines that once ran north to Maryhill Central, east to Partick Central and west to Dumbarton. The CR-style signalbox is to be noted. *R. Nelson*

Below left Just outside Glasgow can be found Clydebank Riverside station, the hexagonal tower, in richly textured red sandstone, on the up platform reflecting the prosperity of this area at the time of construction in 1896. After a period of dereliction following closure in October 1964 the station was turned over to residential use, as seen here in October 2011. *Author's collection*

Left Eglinton Street station, on the line from St Enoch, was renamed Cumberland Street in 1924 and closed in February 1966. The classical columns and pediment of the impressive main entrance, seen here in October 2011, were of red sandstone; the interior made extensive use of white glazed bricks. Although the railway here still saw occasional use, the infrastructure was so overrun with vegetation that it looked more like a lost line. *Author*

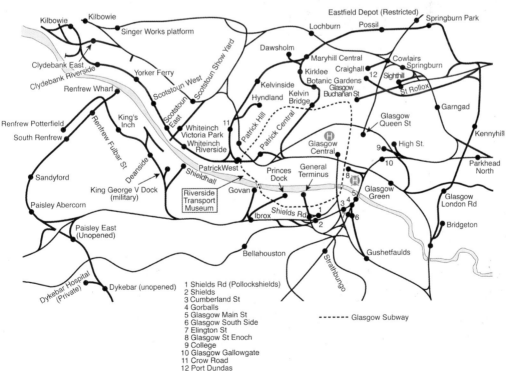

1 Shields Rd (Pollockshields)
2 Shields
3 Cumberland St
4 Gorbals
5 Glasgow Main St
6 Glasgow South Side
7 Elington St
8 Glasgow St Enoch
9 College
10 Glasgow Gallowgate
11 Crow Road
12 Port Dundas

------- Glasgow Subway

The Glasgow goods

A number of early mineral tramways were to be found in the Glasgow area, mainly transporting coal, and the first railway to the city itself, the Garnkirk & Glasgow Railway, opened in 1831, was also intended primarily for freight. Growing trade on the River Clyde meant that for a time goods had to be conveyed through the busy streets between the river quays and the railway depots.

By 1837 the first line was providing direct access to quaysides on the Clyde, and railway connections to Glasgow's growing industries developed steadily thereafter.

The combination of coal, iron ore and the River Clyde saw the building of the *Comet*, the first saltwater commercial steamship to be constructed at Port Glasgow. Such was the growth of steamship construction that at one time about half the world's ships originated from the Clyde area. At its peak there were over 30 shipyards on the Clyde. After World War 1 there was industrial decline, and by the 1930s the Clyde was a depressed area, although the Cunard liners *Queen Mary* and *Queen Elizabeth* were built here. After World War 2 the need to replace merchant shipping, new naval vessels and the building of the *Queen Elizabeth 2* kept the shipyards busy, and this in turn provided continued freight for the railways.

Glasgow was once a focal point for engineering and became the greatest centre for locomotive

Facing page A down freight headed by English Electric Type 1 No D8080 skirts St Rollox shed, between Balornock and Germiston junctions, on 5 January 1963. St Rollox was an ex-CR shed with 12 running roads. Coded 65B, in 1959 it had an allocation of 68 locomotives. It was to close in 1966. *S. Rickard*

Right The CR's original Buchanan Street goods depot was opened in January 1850 and was located beside the passenger station. When this photograph was taken onward road transport was by horse and cart. A new goods depot opened at Buchanan Street in June 1909; this closed in August 1962 and was subsequently demolished. *GPS collection*

construction in Europe. At one time a quarter of all steam locomotives in the world could trace their origins back to Glasgow. The North British Locomotive Co became the most famous. It was created in 1903 by the merger of Dübs & Co, Sharp, Stewart & Co and Neilson, Reid & Co, and although their respective works were retained, a new central administrative block was built at Springburn.

As its industrial might developed in the 19th century Glasgow expanded to the extent that it became known as the 'Second City of Empire'. The growth in rail-borne freight resulted in many of the small early railway goods depots becoming increasingly congested. Consequently, in addition

to stations dealing with both passengers and freight, together with freight connections to many industries and the docks, a number of large goods-only depots were constructed by the pre-Grouping railways.

By World War 1 the Caledonian Railway had the greatest number of goods depots, perhaps the

Below Maryhill Central station goods yard in the 1950s. In addition to the wood and steel in wagons in the yard, destined for industry, a considerable quantity of coal is being bagged for domestic consumption locally; in the yard are three lorries, of which one is clearly a coal lorry. After a period of dereliction following closure the site was redeveloped, but the bridge from which this photograph was taken survives. *Ian Allan Library*

most notable being that adjoining Buchanan Street station, to the north of the river. There were also depots at London Road and Port Dundas. To the south of the river were depots at Eglinton (which became a parcels depot in 1959), Kinning Park and Gushetfaulds. The railway also operated to the General Terminus on the River Clyde.

The Caledonian and Glasgow & South Western railways also had a joint goods depot at Gushetfaulds, besides jointly operating freight lines in the Princes Dock area and other dockside locations on the south bank of the Clyde. The GSWR's huge College Street goods depot was provided with an imposing three-storey stone office block at its entrance. The North British Railway's depots included the equally large High Street goods depot, opened in 1904. The NBR also had goods depots alongside Queen Street passenger station and at Sighthill (close to the CR's St Rollox works), while its Stobcross depot served Queens Dock. In 1923 the ex-NBR goods yards became part of the LNER, the others becoming part of the LMS. Although there were now only two railway companies, there was little rationalisation with

Above Renfrew Wharf, on the south side of the Clyde, on 8 September 1966. By this time there was no name board or building, but the goods depot was still open, and five trains arrived each week. Freight to Renfrew Wharf ceased in June 1967. *C. Thorburn*

Below A Class 08 shunter propels the daily goods working from Partick Central away from the 155yd (142m) Merkland Street Tunnel and uphill towards Yoker Yard, some 4 miles away, in February 1977. This remnant of the former Glasgow Central Railway was not electrified and was closed in October 1978. Below Merkland Street Tunnel can still be found the disused Merkland Street station, on the Glasgow subway. *G. Offana*

Above Shunting wagons by tractor at Glasgow's Sighthill freight terminal, on 1 July 1962. At this time onward delivery would have been undertaken by a fleet of BR lorries. The terminal closed in October 1981, and the site has since been redeveloped as a business park. *BR*

regard to goods facilities. In 1948 all the competing yards were consolidated within the Scottish Region of the newly formed British Railways.

The 1960s were to see further large-scale decline in Glasgow's industrial might. The North British Locomotive Co had built mighty steam locomotives that were exported around the world, but when it turned to producing diesel locomotives these proved unreliable, and the firm went bankrupt in 1962.

Rail-borne freight at Glasgow suffered from the decline of the city's industries, combined with increased road competition and changes proposed as part of BR's 1955 Modernisation Plan, which included construction of a marshalling yard at Cadder, to the northeast of Glasgow. Buchanan Street goods depot closed in August 1962, and that at Queen Street in January 1964. High Street and College goods yards closed in 1968, and the 1960s saw the closure of most of the other goods depots in central Glasgow. Iron-ore trains to Ravenscraig steelworks ceased running from the General Terminus in 1979, while 1984 witnessed the closure of one of the last general goods yards, at London Road depot. Scotland's first Freightliner depot, at Gushetfaulds, was opened in 1965 on the site of the earlier goods depot but closed in 1993, replaced by other freight facilities further away from central Glasgow.

Despite all the changes and closures there are still freight workings in and around Glasgow, while evidence remains of some of the former goods facilities, and short sections of derelict track are to be found throughout the area.

Below Map showing the LMS College Street and LNER High Street goods depots at Glasgow in 1926. *Crown copyright*

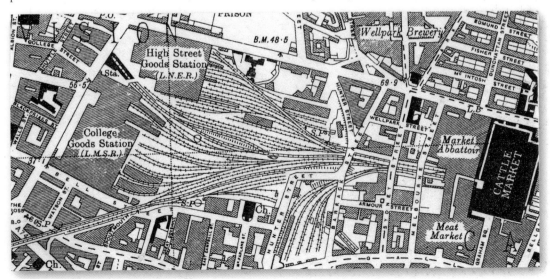

Facing page Greenock Princes Pier signalbox disappears behind a cloud of smoke and steam as preserved HR 4-6-0 No 103 leaves with an SLS/RCTS Easter railtour on 17 April 1965. *P. Riley*

Left Extensive freight facilities developed, notably the ex-GSWR College Street goods depot, which at one time was connected to the bonded whisky warehouse at Bell Street. Bell Street was opened in 1883, also by the GSWR, and, although stone-clad, has concrete and cast-iron floors. The warehouse was a very early example of the bulk use of concrete. This huge building, occupying 200,000sq ft (18,580sq m), is now used as apartments, as seen here in September 2010. *Author*

Below left When the rest of High Street goods depot was demolished the wall facing Duke Street, built of red brick and yellow stone, was retained, and much of it has now been attractively incorporated into a new development. A section of the considerable length of wall is seen here in October 2011. *Author*

Above The John Brown shipyard, which built the *Queen Mary*, *Queen Elizabeth* and QE2. Although there has been much redevelopment nearby, the shipyard area, once served by the ex-CR line to Dumbarton, lay derelict in 2009. The photograph was taken from the top of a restored Titan crane, now a tourist attraction, showing how adept Glasgow has been at reinventing itself. *Author*

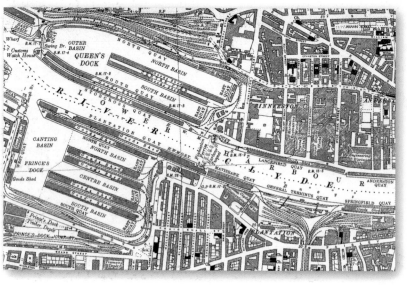

Left Map of goods lines adjoining the River Clyde and dock basins at Glasgow in 1926. *Crown copyright*

8

Beside the Clyde

The River Clyde served as a gateway to mainland Scotland from the Western Isles, Ireland and far-flung ports of the world, and from the 1840s regular transatlantic sailings were introduced. The Clyde also developed as an important pleasure route 'doon the watter', and a fleet of paddle steamers, both railway and independently owned, plied their trade along the river.

Greenock developed as a significant port on the Lower Clyde. The ex-CR line from Glasgow to Greenock remains open, but the rival ex-GSWR line to Greenock Princes Pier is closed.

The Princes Pier line opened in December 1869, when the station was known as Greenock Albert Harbour (a name it retained until 1875). Trains travelled the 26 miles to and from Glasgow and for a while also ran directly from Edinburgh, to the consternation of the CR, which had opposed the competing route. The CR tried to persuade

steamboat operators to boycott its new rival, but when this failed it retimed trains serving its nearby Custom House Quay to cause maximum delay to steamers continuing to Princes Pier; this plan also failed and simply resulted in more steamers calling only at Princes Pier.

Princes Pier station was located next to the quayside and was thus far more convenient than the CR pier at Custom House Quay, which required a steep walk up to the CR's Greenock Central station. Princes Pier soon became the more popular station, and, besides local services on the Clyde, steamers provided a daily service to Ireland. Goods sidings also connected to the adjoining Albert Harbour, and freight traffic developed on the route.

After a time the rival companies came to work pragmatically together in the operation of Clyde steamboats. However, in 1889 the CR opened a new line to Gourock, which became more important, eclipsing Princes Pier, much as the latter had earlier eclipsed Custom House Quay. In retaliation the GSWR built a distinctive and imposing new Princes Pier station, in a 'Spanish style', this opening in 1894. Priority was given to boat trains, new steamers were provided, and some trade was regained.

When the LMS took over both lines to Greenock it began a process of paring down the once-competing Clyde services. The Clydebank blitz caused much damage in the Greenock area, but

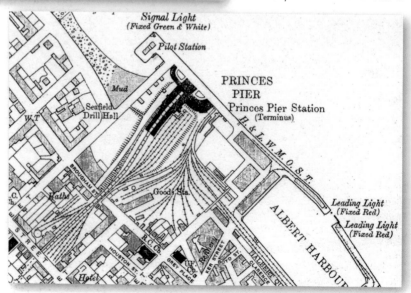

the line was busy with American troops arriving at the port during World War 2. After the war its use diminished, and the duplication of services could not continue. BR took over in 1948 and in 1952 rationalised services, connecting steamboats to and from Princes Pier being withdrawn. The section of line between Princes Pier and Kilmacolm closed to regular passenger services in 1959. However, Princes Pier remained as an Ocean Liner terminal, and passengers continued to be transported to and from Glasgow in boat trains until November 1965; freight traffic ceased in September of the following year. The remaining 8-mile single line from the east of Paisley to Kilmacolm was a

Steamer Sailings between Scotland and Ireland
Via Greenock and via Ardrossan (Burns and Laird Lines Ltd).

All Sailings and Train connections are subject to alteration without notice and should be verified beforehand at the Shipping Company's Office, 58 Robertson Street, Glasgow, C.2

	A a.m.		p.m	p.m				A p.m	p.m	p.m
Glasgow (Central) lev.	8 25	..	..	..	..	Londonderry ... lev.	..	..	7 B 0	..	..
Glasgow (St. Enoch) ..	..	..	5 7	6 30	..	Dublin	..	..	..	..	6 B 30
Paisley (Gil. St.) ...	8 38	..	5c24	6c56	..	Belfast	..	3 45	..	..	..
Greenock	..	..	..	..	..	Ardrossan	..	..	..	..	..
Princes Pier .. arr.	..	..	6 5	7 39	..	(Montgomerie Pr) arr.	7 45	..	..	..	..
Ardrossan	..	..	..	..	..	Greenock (Princes P) ..	..	..	5 E 0	8 E 0	..
(Montgomerie Pr)	9 13	..	..	..	..	Ardrossan	..	..	..	..	..
Greenock (Princes P) lev	..	..	6 30	8 0	..	(Montgomerie Pr) lev.	8 15	..	..	..	..
Ardrossan	..	..	..	..	..	Greenock	..	..	..	..	..
(Montgomerie Pr) ..	9 45	..	a.m.	..	..	(Princes Pier)	..	..	7 E 35	8 E 20	..
Belfast .... arr. abt.	1p45	..	8 0	..	..	Paisley (Gil. St.) ...	8 53	..	8 E 15	8c59 E	..
Dublin	..	..	..	a.m.	..	Glasgow (Central) arr.	9 6	..	..	..	..
Londonderry	..	..	..	6 30	..	Glasgow (St. Enoch)	..	..	8 E 33	9 E 14	..

A Weekdays; 17th June until 9th Sept. inclusive, also on Sundays 16th and 30th July and 13th August
B Wednesdays only   c Canal Station   E Thursday mornings

Above Timetable of Irish boat trains to and from Princes Pier in the summer of 1950.

Right Map of Princes Pier station at Greenock in 1912. *Crown copyright*

late survivor, passenger services being withdrawn as recently as January 1983.

The Princes Pier station buildings were demolished, but after a number of years of disuse the site was redeveloped as a container terminal, a short freight link at Greenock being laid from the

Wemyss Bay line in 1971 to connect with the original alignment. Some tracks to the site of Princes Pier still remained *in situ* in 2011 but were incomplete and had not been used for freight since 1991. Elsewhere parts of the former trackbed are used as the basis of a cycleway.

Right Fairburn 2-6-4T No 2190 with a Glasgow train at Greenock Princes Pier on 18 April 1949. Although the railways had been nationalised a year previously, the locomotive was yet to receive its BR number. *J. Henton*

Below Headed by BR Standard Class 4 2-6-0 No 76099, a Greenock Princes Pier–Glasgow St Enoch train crosses Cartsburn Viaduct on 8 November 1958. The 'boat trains' continued to use the line after the regular passenger service to Princes Pier was withdrawn in 1959. The viaduct remains *in situ* following final closure of this section of line in 1966. *G. Robin*

Left BR Standard Class 4 2-6-4T No 80128 on the 5.36pm Glasgow St Enoch–Kilmacolm service at Kilmacolm station in August 1965. The platform canopies were later demolished, but the distinctive GSWR signalbox would survive until 1973, when the remaining passenger stub to Kilmacolm was singled. *R. Ruffell*

Facing page Still in LNER livery, ex-NBR Class C16 4-4-2T No 7500 approaches Blanefield with an Aberfoyle–Glasgow train in July 1948. For a while in the 1930s the LNER had used Sentinel steam railcars on the line. The woods remain, as do some small remains of Blanefield station. *P. Alexander*

Above A short length of overgrown track can just be discerned in this leafy glade in the heart of Greenock, photographed in September 2010. Beyond the bridge the line led to Ann Street Tunnel. *Author*

Above right The line from Princes Pier, on the banks of the River Clyde, was on a rising gradient and required two tunnels under Greenock. The deep western entrance to the 420yd (384m) Ann Street Tunnel, on the approach to Greenock Lynedoch station, is seen here in September 2010 from Mearns Street Bridge. Mearns Street signalbox was once perched in the cutting on the left. *Author*

Right The approach to Princes Pier was redeveloped as a freight container depot with a new rail access to the Wemyss Bay line. The depot is seen here in September 2010, out of use, but with the *Queen Victoria*, making her maiden visit to the port, as a backdrop. Significant maritime events on the Clyde are usually attended by the Clyde-built ex-LNER paddle steamer *Waverley*, and this was no exception. *Author*

Left The site of Greenock's elegant Princes Pier station, viewed from deck of the *Queen Elizabeth 2* in September 2007. Launched in 1967, the QE2 was to be the last of the Clyde-built ocean liners. This visit marked her 40th birthday, and former John Brown shipyard workers were invited to visit the ship, which was destined to be taken out of service the following year. *Author*

9

Cross-country casualties

The more rural parts of central Scotland were served by various lengthy cross-country lines. Some of these had been built primarily to gain access to mineral deposits and ran passenger trains as a secondary consideration; others relied more on passenger services, but these were often of a seasonal nature or used shorter sections of line. All were secondary routes that became increasingly vulnerable once the supremacy of rail was challenged by road transport.

To the north of Glasgow the railway reached Aberfoyle in October 1882, enabling Glaswegians to escape their then grimy city and travel some 34¼ miles across country to this summer bridgehead for tours of the Trossachs. Services were worked by the NBR, and through trains to and from Glasgow also served the Blane Valley. In later years most trains terminated at Blanefield, and on weekdays a connecting service of two trains in each direction ran to and from Aberfoyle, often with very few passengers. The line closed to passengers on 29 September 1951, when so many wanted to travel that Glasgow Queen Street ran out of tickets. Freight to Aberfoyle ceased in October 1959 but survived on the southern section to Lennoxtown until April 1966.

To the south of Glasgow a network of GSWR lines developed around Kilmarnock, with links (now closed) via Crosshouse to the Ayrshire coast. Striking

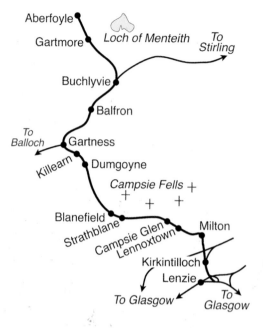

ore and coal deposits had been a key reason for the lines in the Strathaven area, the Strathaven–Darvel section passed through remote farmland and closed to all traffic in September 1939. Passenger services between Strathaven and Hamilton via Quarter were withdrawn by the LMS in October 1945, and in September 1953 remaining freight traffic ceased. Passenger and freight services on the Hurlford–Darvel line ceased in April 1964. Passenger services between Strathaven and Hamilton via Stonehouse were withdrawn in October 1965, freight having ceased the previous year.

The GSWR's 12¼-mile Auchinleck–Muirkirk line opened in August 1848. A 19-mile CR extension to Lanark opened in January 1873, for goods traffic only, passenger services commencing in June of the following year. Through services to Ayr did not commence until June 1878. Together the lines provided a secondary cross-country route from the Ayrshire coast to Lanark, but there were very few through trains, and passenger numbers were limited. By contrast freight traffic, particularly coal, was at one time heavy, and a link was provided to the

eastward, the GSWR opened the 7¼-mile Hurlford–Darvel line in June 1896, and the CR extended the line some 11 miles to Strathaven, this section opening in May 1905. From here two further CR lines ran to Hamilton, via Quarter and via Stonehouse. Although the GSWR and CR both worked trains over the Darvel–Strathaven section and both had booking offices at Strathaven, there were no through passenger trains on the entire route. While iron-

Below The last day of passenger working at Lennoxtown, 29 September 1951. Most services terminated here, and empty stock is passing the signalbox for reversal, headed by ex-NBR Class J37 0-6-0 No 64639, the highest-numbered (by BR) in a series of 104 locomotives built 1914-21. Lenzie–Lennoxtown freight ceased in April 1966. *G. Robin*

Coalburn branch. However, the Auchinleck–Lanark line was never developed as a through route because the CR was concerned that the GSWR might seek to extend its running powers eastward to Lanark. Muirkirk once had six collieries and an iron industry. The ironworks closed in 1923, and by 1934 only one coalmine remained. The last passenger train from Auchinleck to Muirkirk ran in September 1951, while the Lanark–Muirkirk service was withdrawn in October 1964. Freight on the remaining Lanark–Ponfeigh section survived until January 1968.

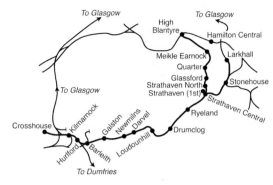

DARVEL and STRATHAVEN (3rd class only).—Glasgow and South Western and Caledonian.																		
Miles	**Down.**		**Week Days.**						Miles	**Up.**			**Week Days.**					
		mrn	aft							Central Station,		mrn	aft					
	Darvel .... dep.	6 10	7 25							Strathaven .... dep.		8 15	5 15					
2¾	Loudounhill	6 25	7 40						3¾	Ryeland		8 35	5 50					
5¾	Drumclog	6 40	7 55						5¾	Drumclog		8 53	6 15					
7¾	Ryeland	7 0	8 15						8¼	Loudounhill		9 12	6 35					
11	Strathaven (Cen.) 879, 880 arr.	7 15	8 40						11	Darvel 843 .... arr.		9 27	6 52					

Above Darvel–Strathaven timetable, April 1910.

Left Kirkintilloch on 6 July 1963, with English Electric Type 1 No D8092 shunting a freight train from Lennoxtown and a Metro-Cammell DMU returning to Glasgow, having arrived as the 11.45am from Queen Street. Passenger services on this short remaining stub from Lenzie remained until September 1964, while freight survived until April 1966. *L. Sandler*

Left Ex-LMS Class 2P 4-4-0 No 40638 entering Crosshouse with the 3.12pm Adrossan–Darvel train on 22 May 1961. All passenger services here ceased in April 1966. The lines on the left of this view were the first to be removed, followed by those on the right, after final closure to freight in October 1973. Today little remains. *D. Butterfield*

Left Ex-CR 'Jumbo' 0-6-0 No 57295 heading the 9.50am Darvel–Kilmarnock train near Galston on 5 September 1960. The rostered locomotive, a BR Standard Class 5, had failed at Darvel, so the train was cancelled and worked as empty stock. *D. Lane*

Right Strathaven station on 24 April 1963, with a Cravens DMU having arrived as the 5.50pm from Stonehouse. The elegant ex-CR buildings have long gone since closure, but the remains of the island platform could still be found in 2010. *L. Sandler*

Left The closed Quarter station viewed in the direction of Strathaven on 28 April 1956. Passenger services between Hamilton and Strathaven via Quarter were withdrawn in October 1945, and regular freight ceased in September 1953, although the track would not be not removed until 1959. The nearby station house remains. *W. Smith*

Left A Gloucester RCW two-car DMU at Muirkirk, forming the 13.30 to Lanark, on Saturday 3 October 1964, the last day of service. The station was located in the centre of a hive of industry, notably coal mining, and even boasted a locomotive shed, which closed on the same day. *J. Haydon*

Left The bleak and remote station at Inches on 3 October 1964, the last day of service on this part of the line between Muirkirk and Ponfeigh, which was subsequently abandoned completely. Today nothing remains of Inches station. *D. Smith*

Left A Cravens DMU stands at Coalburn on 24 April 1963, having arrived as of the 4.15pm from Hamilton. At one time workmen's trains continued beyond the station to Bankend Colliery, but this section closed to all traffic in 1963. The line provided a link to the Auchinleck–Lanark line but was never used as a through route. All remaining services to Coalburn would be withdrawn in September 1965. *L. Sandler*

Below Preserved ex-GNSR Class D40 4-4-0 *Gordon Highlander* on the single-track branch from Lanark to Ponfeigh with a Branch Line Society special train, on Saturday 16 October 1965. This section of the line remained open for freight until January 1968. After final closure the viaduct over the River Clyde was demolished. *R. Fisher*

10

Suburban Edinburgh

Edinburgh's hilly topography and its historic buildings caused complications for railway construction in the city, but a network of suburban commuter services was duly established. The Edinburgh and Leith trams were more limited in their routes and not as fast as those in Glasgow, so for many years the suburban railways of the Scottish capital prospered.

In the 1920s Waverley station alone dispatched almost 100 suburban services daily, and Princes Street more than 60. By the mid-1960s, and without significant protest, buses and cars had mostly replaced the inner-suburban trains and the trams. As a consequence just a few suburban stations remain.

The first passenger service was provided on the southern outskirts of the city by the Edinburgh & Dalkeith Railway (E&DR), which in July 1831 introduced a horse-worked St Leonards–

Craighill service. This proved a great success, and the prospect of passengers ambling along by Holyrood Park, the absence of fatalities (contrasting with experiences elsewhere) and a relaxed management gave rise to its being dubbed 'the Innocent Railway'. Other routes were duly added, including a circuitous line to Leith. The railway was taken over by the NBR in 1845 and brought up to main-line standards, but with the construction of new and more central lines, passenger services at St

Above The 566yd (517m) tunnel at St Leonards was the first on a public passenger railway in Scotland. Built on a 1-in-30 grade, which at one time required a stationary engine to haul stock, the double-track tunnel was originally lit by gas. It still survives, and the sandstone southern portal is seen here in September 2010. Today it is lit by electricity and used as a cycleway and footpath. *Author*

Facing page Ex-NBR Class J36 0-6-0 No 65345 crossing the River Esk as it arrives at Musselburgh with an RCTS special on 27 August 1966. By this time the branch had closed to passengers, in September 1964, but freight would continue until 1971. The bridge survives today, having been converted for road use, but nothing remains of the station. *J. Bird*

Leonards ceased in November 1847, this being the first withdrawal of a passenger service in the city.

To the north, a passenger line from Scotland Street to Trinity opened, in part, during August 1842. Construction of the 1,000yd (914m) Scotland Street Tunnel underneath the ridge of Edinburgh New Town met with considerable opposition, and the Canal Street– Granton/Leith lines were not all fully operational until 1847. Carriages on the steepest part of the line, out of Canal Street, were rope-hauled by a stationary steam engine, but this proved less than satisfactory, and the station and tunnel closed in March 1868 when an alternative route from Waverley, via Abbeyhill, was opened. Passenger services on the Granton section were withdrawn abruptly by the LNER in November 1925.

To the east, the 3-mile Musselburgh branch opened in July 1847, using part of the ex-E&DR Fisherrow line. It developed a suburban service but closed to passengers in September 1964 and to freight in September 1971.

To the southwest, the 6-mile Balerno loop opened in 1874. Prior to World War 1 passenger traffic was

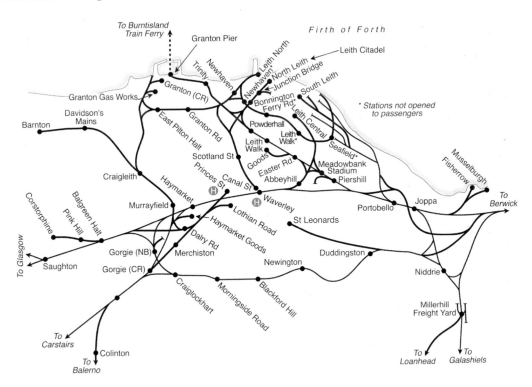

EDINBURGH and LEITH.—North British.—2 miles.

Edinburgh (Waverley) to Leith (Central) every half-hour from 5 40 mrn. to 11 10 aft.
Leith (Central) to Edinburgh (Waverley) every half-hour from 5 55 mrn. to 11 25 aft.

heavy, and in September 1927 Hailes Platform was added to serve a local golf club. By World War 2 traffic had declined, and passenger services were suspended by the LMS in November 1943, never to be resumed. Freight survived longer, until December 1967.

In February 1902 the 3-mile branch to Corstorphine opened to serve developing suburbs to the west of the city, the utilitarian terminus opening in the same year as the North British Hotel at Waverley station, which is one of Edinburgh's grandest and most romantic buildings. Pinkhill, the original intermediate station on the branch, closed as a temporary World War 1 economy measure in 1917, reopening in 1919; Balgreen Halt was added in January 1934. The line closed in December 1967.

Leith was the main port located north of Edinburgh, and the Caledonian and North British railways, Corporation trams and SMT buses all vied with each other to serve the area and link it with the city centre. Nevertheless, by the early 1920s railways from Leith provided more Edinburgh commuters than any other destination.

The NBR at one time had three passenger termini at Leith, the first being served by the E&DR route opened in July 1838 to South Leith. This was also the first line to be closed to regular passenger services by the NBR, in 1903, although part of it remains for freight.

The second link, to North Leith (or Leith Citadel, as the station would later be renamed by BR, to help prevent confusion with the ex-CR station at Leith North), was opened in May 1846. A steam railmotor was used by the LNER from 1929; nevertheless the line was closed to passenger services in June 1947 and to all traffic in February 1968, although a short section as far as Powderhall remains open to freight.

The NBR's last new suburban line was the 2-mile branch, opened for passengers in July 1903, to a huge new terminus at Leith Central. Although this was Leith's most direct suburban railway, the steps up from Waverley station to Princes Street are said to be partly to blame for its early demise. It closed

Above Edinburgh–Leith Central timetable, April 1910.

Below The passenger station at Granton was located on the Middle Pier and is seen here with naval personnel on the platform. The single wooden platform and station building were early victims of closure; to considerable public objection the LNER gave just 10 days' notice, in October 1925. There are no remains of the station today. *J. Sutherland*

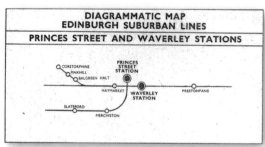

DIAGRAMMATIC MAP
EDINBURGH SUBURBAN LINES
PRINCES STREET AND WAVERLEY STATIONS

Above BR map showing the remnants of the Edinburgh suburban lines in 1965.

to passengers in April 1952, the station area at Leith Central being converted to a diesel depot, itself destined to be closed in April 1972.

The CR's circuitous 5½-mile Princes Street–Leith North branch opened for passengers in August 1879. In March 1894 a branch also opened to Barnton. East Pilton was given a halt in December 1934 to encourage residents of a new housing estate to use the line. The line to Barnton closed in May 1951, while the rest of the line closed to passengers in April 1962 and to freight in 1967. Princes Street station itself was the largest station in Scotland closed on Beeching's recommendation, in September 1965.

Edinburgh's suburban rail services were gradually decimated, and such was the extent of the closures that a network of cycle routes has been established using the former lines. Yet there is still rail commuting into the city, mostly now from outer rather than inner areas. A number of new stations on existing lines in the Edinburgh area have been provided, and services to Newcraighall were reintroduced in 1992. Even tram lines have returned to Princes Street!

Left A Musselburgh–Edinburgh passenger train headed by Gresley-designed Class V3 2-6-2T No 67670 passes busy goods sidings between Musselburgh and Fisherrow Junction on 20 July 1951. The branch was double-track, and DMUs were introduced from 1958, but passenger services would be withdrawn in 1964. *W. Turnbull*

Left Colinton station, on the Balerno branch, with the 'Scottish Rambler 4' of 19 April 1965, hauled by BR Standard Class 2 2-6-0 No 78046. Behind the train is the 135yd (123m) Colinton Tunnel. The wooden station buildings are just visible through the steam to the left of the locomotive. Much of the branch and the tunnel is now a cycle route. *D. Idle*

Right The Corstorphine terminus in July 1954, with ex-LNER Class D49 4-4-0 No 62715 *Roxburghshire* heading a train for Edinburgh Waverley. The 12-minute journey time to or from Waverley station would become a thing of the past with the closure of this last suburban branch in the Edinburgh area, in December 1967. *Ian Allan Library*

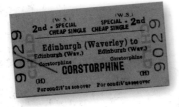

Below Ex-LNER Class V3 2-6-2T No 67615 heading a seven-coach train out of Pinkhill on 23 January 1960. Note the gas-lit road. The station buildings and platform still remain, while the former trackbed is used as a footpath. The station served Edinburgh Zoo. *G. Staddon*

Below right Pinkhill station buildings still remained in June 2011. Nowadays used as a garage, they were boarded up before the line closed, and it is said locally that they once housed the railway's local rat catcher. Foliage has consumed the area since the railway closed, but much of the Corstorphine branch is today used as a footpath and cycleway. *Author*

Left South Leith on 25 August 1962, with Class V3 2-6-2T No 67668 heading a railtour. This was the first station at Leith, opened in 1832, 'South' being added in 1859 following the opening of other stations in the area. The station closed to regular passenger services when Leith Central opened. *G. Staddon*

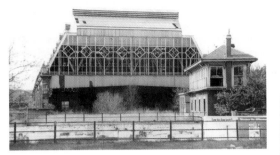

Above The huge and rather ungainly trainshed and the 81-lever-frame signalbox at Leith Central, seen in derelict condition in April 1987. The station had closed to passengers in April 1952, after less than 50 years of use, following which the trainshed was used as a diesel maintenance depot, until this itself closed in 1972. The trainshed would be demolished 1989, but the stone frontage of the station remains, as does the clock tower. *A. Mullay*

Left Dating from 1846, North Leith – or Leith Citadel, as it was also known, to avoid confusion with Leith North – is the only significant railway terminus building to survive at Leith. Passenger services ceased in 1947, and freight in 1968. Nowadays a listed building, it was designed by Grainger & Miller in a classical style incorporating numerous columns both round, as seen here in June 2011, and square, all attractively decorated with acanthus leaves and harebells. *Author*

Above The Leith North terminus on 14 April 1962, with driver F. Minay standing proudly by the DMU. Following the withdrawal of passenger services at the end of the month the covered trainshed survived as a store for many years before the site was redeveloped as housing. Suburban services on the ex-CR line to Leith lasted longer than those on the ex-NBR lines, arguably because of the ground-level convenience of Princes Street station – as opposed to the numerous steps up from Waverley. *G. Staddon*

Right Ex-CR 0-6-0 No 57559 at Craigleith with the 1.43pm train from Leith North on 30 April 1958; the Barton branch can be seen diverging to the left. Today the junction area is overgrown with mature trees, but the former trackbed here is used as a footpath, and the site of the station, with its platform edges, is readily identifiable. *G. Staddon*

Above Ex-CR Class 2P 0-4-4T No 55229 at Murrayfield with a Leith North–Princes Street train on 11 March 1958. Snow remains on the platform edges, most of which are still to be found on the site today. *G. Staddon*

Right The ornamental bridge abutment at Murrayfield, alongside the A8 road, seen in June 2011. The elegant stone abutments incorporate the initials 'CR', while the central part of the bridge includes emblems of Scotland – a thistle and lions rampant. The former trackbed is now used as a footpath and cycleway. *Author*

Facing page Even some of the most modern rail-borne freight has been lost. Here Class 37 No 37 147 prepares to run round its train of naphtha wagons from the Texaco sidings at Granton before departing for Grangemouth on 26 September 1978. This line was little used after 1980, and from 1986 it was cut back to Powderhall. *M. Macdonald*

Above Ex-CR 0-4-4T No 55233 on a Leith local leaving Princes Street in wintry conditions. DMUs were introduced in the late 1950s, but Leith services from Princes Street ceased in 1962. Princes Street itself closed in 1965, its demise being described in *Lost Lines: Scotland. Ian Allan Library*

Right The Caledonian Hotel at Princes Street remains, but the station itself has been demolished and redeveloped. The former main line out of Princes Street has been turned into a road, as seen here in September 2010. *Author*

11

Freight losses in the Lothians

In 1722 the first goods line with a clear provenance in Scotland ran between Tranent and Cockenzie harbour on the Firth of Forth. It was a horse-operated waggonway, originally laid down with wooden tracks to convey coal. The waggonway was even involved in the Battle of Prestonpans during the Jacobite Rebellion of 1745. Iron rails were used after 1815, and in 1880 it became part of a colliery network. The line closed in 1959, although a section remained for wagon storage until 1963.

In 1831 a line opened from Edinburgh St Leonards to coal mines to the southeast of Edinburgh in the Dalhousie area. Edinburgh's growth and ever-increasing need for coal resulted in this early link with the Midlothian coalfield. Further extensions were added to these 4ft 6in 'Scottish gauge' lines, and for many years wagons were drawn by horses. The commercial success of the lines saw a goods network develop serving the Midlothian coalfield, Leith and the fishing port of Fisherrow. The routes were later taken over by the NBR and rebuilt to standard gauge.

A deep-water harbour was built at Granton, and in 1850 the world's first 'modern' train ferry began operating. It was used to transport up to 40 goods wagons across the Firth of Forth to Burntisland. Designed by Thomas Grainger, the ferry was built

on the Clyde by Robert Napier & Sons. Operation of the freight ferry ceased with the opening of the Forth Bridge in 1890, although an LNER passenger ferry continued until World War 2. Rail-borne freight to Granton ceased in 1986.

The expansion of Leith Docks, notably the opening of Edinburgh Dock in 1881 for coal exports, presented lucrative goods traffic for the railways. Leith became the second port of Scotland, and the network of NBR and CR dock lines was kept busy. The CR's extension to Seafield was one of the last lines opened, in 1903. A passenger service was originally proposed, but competition from nearby NBR stations and from the trams ensured that the branch was only ever used for goods. It marked a turning-point in the continuous growth of the railways in the area.

Edinburgh, as the capital of Scotland, with an emphasis on banking and service industries, had less heavy industry than Glasgow. Nevertheless there

Above Ex-NBR Class J88 0-6-0T No 68340 with loaded wagons at Granton Square on 29 August 1955. It was from the Middle Pier at Granton that the first mixed-goods train ferry operated to Burntisland. The ferry service was withdrawn upon the opening of the Forth Bridge in 1890. *G. Staddon*

were industries that were well established, including brewing, printing and the manufacture of paper, glass bottles and glue, to name but a few. Most were served by rail links and sidings, all of which have closed.

In the late 1950s an extensive marshalling yard was built at Millerhill, on the southeast outskirts of Edinburgh. This was intended to replace smaller yards, although its construction ignored the declining number of wagonloads being sent by rail. The yard became fully operational in 1963. It did result in the closure of smaller goods yards at Niddrie, Joppa, Portobello and Hardengreen and was for a while a success, about 4,000 wagons a day using the facility. In 1969 closure of the Waverley route led to the closure

Right Ex-NBR Class J83 0-6-0T No 68448 at South Leith on 3 October 1953. 'LGW' on the pitched-roofed grain wagons, used for whisky production, denotes Leith General Warehousing; the wagons ran from Leith Docks to Haymarket goods depot. *G. Staddon*

of the up sidings, while the down sidings survived until 1983. Today small parts of the yard are still used for various rail and freight activities.

The 1960s saw extensive freight closures in the area, from goods-only lines to individual station yards and main goods depots. They included all the principal goods depots in Edinburgh, most of which also handled coal. Lothian Road depot, just outside Princes Street, saw its rail freight cease in September 1964. Haymarket goods yard, in Morrison Street, closed in August 1966, while Waverley goods depot closed at the end of 1966. Scotland Street, for many years used exclusively as a coal depot, closed in 1967, while Leith Walk, St Leonards and Bonnington depots followed in May, August and December 1968.

To the west of Edinburgh, in the West Lothian area, oil was once extracted from deposits of shale, and a network of lines developed to serve both this and the coal industry. These peaked prior to World War 1, following which the network saw years of contraction, the extraction of shale oil finally ceasing in 1962. Some of the last coal lines to close included that to Lower Bathgate, which remained open to serve Easton Colliery until 1974. The last deep mine in the area closed a decade later.

To the southeast of Edinburgh, in the the Midlothian coalfield, Smeaton Colliery (near Dalkeith) and its line closed in 1978. In 1989 the line to Bilston Glen Colliery closed, while Monktonhall, served by the same network of lines, was one of the

Above Two ex-NBR Class Y9 0-4-0STs, Nos 68102 and 68095 (the latter now preserved), pictured at Seafield. These locomotives' short wheelbase made them ideal for the tight curves in the docks, but the limited capacity of their coal bunkers necessitated the use of four-wheeled wooden wagons as coal tenders. The locomotive shed at Seafield was closed in 1962 and was demolished in 1966. *T. Booth*

last rail-connected pits to close, in 1997. In East Lothian the Blindwells opencast pit commenced extraction in 1978, and a new line was laid, connecting it to the East Coast main line. This link was little used after 2000, and the track was lifted in 2010, although, bizarrely, colour-light signals remained in place in 2011.

Coal is still transported by rail in the Lothians and, in an extraordinary reversal of history, is now *imported* via Leith Docks, ensuring that part of the very first railway route to serve the port continues to be used for freight.

Left Pictured on the Figgate Burn bridge, elderly ex-NBR Class Y9 0-4-0 No 68119 shunts at the United Glass bottle works at Portobello on 30 May 1959. The works had two oil-fired furnaces, and trains brought in fuel, sand and chemicals. The introduction of plastic bottles led to the closure of the factory in 1967. *G. Staddon*

Above Ex-NBR Class J88 0-6-0T No 68335 shunts in the siding to the Gorgie Mills factory in Edinburgh. Gorgie Mills made glue, and coal was required to heat the boiling cauldrons of animal bones used in the glue-making process. The works closed in 1969. *The Rev R. Hughes*

Right Adjacent to Princes Street station, Lothian Road was originally a wooden-built passenger station, but following a fire in 1890 it was rebuilt as the CR's main goods depot in central Edinburgh. Rail-borne freight ceased in September 1964, and track on the left had already been lifted by the time this photograph was taken from the roof of the Usher Hall. *A. McLean*

Left Ex-NBR Class J36 0-6-0 No 65282 leaves Wood End Colliery for Bathgate in March 1964. The colliery closed the following year, but the washery was retained for a while longer to treat coal from other local collieries. Note the slag-heap (known locally as a 'bing') in the background. *M. Pope*

Left Class J36 0-6-0 No 65319 shunts at Riddochhill Colliery, near Bathgate, on 1 June 1966. The colliery closed in 1968, and the M8 motorway was subsequently built over the site. *L. Nixon*

Below Pictured on the Loanhead branch east of Gilmerton on 8 September 1977, Class 26 No 26006 heads a merry-go-round coal train between Bilston Glen Colliery and Cockenzie power station. By 1989 the colliery had closed, but the branch was being used to clear coal stocks. Disused tracks remained in the 1990s, but parts of the branch are now used as footpaths. *M. Macdonald*

Right The view from the cab of Class J36 No 65234 at St Margarets shed (64A) in September 1965. The locomotive put in more than 60 years of service, thereafter being used as a stationary boiler until closure of the shed in 1967. As can be seen, a number of new 'Clayton' Type 1 diesels had been allocated for freight work in the area. In stark contrast with their forebears, these locomotives would remain in service for barely six years. *Author*

Facing page Class B1 4-6-0 No 61133 at Leven with the 10.35am Saturdays-only Crail–Edinburgh train, on 4 July 1964. The Leven–St Andrews section closed in September 1965. Leven was the junction for the line along the coast to Thornton Junction via Methil and the Wemyss Coal Co lines, the latter of which survived until 1970. The coast line closed to passengers in January 1955, while general freight ceased in 1966. *C. Thornburn*

Above A preserved Leith General Warehousing covered grain hopper wagon in the Scottish Railway Exhibition at Bo'ness in June 2011. Built in Motherwell in 1903, it is the last survivor of a large fleet of 10-ton wagons run by the company. *Author's collection*

Above right Old coal wagons at Prestongrange Museum in East Lothian, seen in June 2011. Thousands of these wagons would have once served the collieries in the area. The museum occupies the site of a colliery and various inter-related industries and provides a reminder not only of surface railways but of the narrow-gauge underground colliery lines. *Author*

Right First and last. The Tranent–Cockenzie Waggonway opened in 1772, and the trackbed is still clearly visible in parts. North of Cockenzie a section of the 2½-mile route that was used to transport coal to the coast on a descending gradient is now used as a footpath, as seen here in June 2011. *Author*

12

Steaming on the Fife coast

The peninsula between the Firth of Forth and Firth of Tay is known as the Kingdom of Fife. It is also the home of golf, and the ancient university town of St Andrews is one of the most significant and best-known settlements in Scotland.

The first railway to serve the area was the 5-mile line between Leuchars and St Andrews, opened in July 1852. It was built economically, by cutting corners, under the auspices of Thomas Bouch, the engineer of the ill-fated Tay Bridge. To the south, the line from Thornton Junction to Leven opened in July 1854 and by September 1863 had been extended to Anstruther. By May 1887 an NBR line linked Anstruther to St Andrews, completing a 34-mile route around the Fife coast from Thornton Junction and encompassing a new through station at St Andrews, the original now being used for goods traffic.

In terms of freight, fish was important, and St Andrews once had nearly 60 fishing boats. St Andrews University and tourism also boosted revenues. In addition, commuting developed from the picturesque coastal fishing villages. Stations were very busy prior to World War 2, and views of the line reveal that, even until closure in 1969, it was well used, particularly on summer Saturdays, when additional trains ran.

A noteworthy train on the line was the 'Fife Coast Express'; one train ran from Edinburgh, and another from Glasgow, some terminating at Crail. For a time they used carriages displaced from the prewar 'Silver Jubilee', and the Edinburgh train even boasted a restaurant car. Some Edinburgh–Dundee trains also ran via the coast.

The Leuchars–St Andrews section is recorded in the Beeching report as having 10,000 passengers a week, and today St Andrews has a population in excess of 16,000, its student population making it one of the most important towns in Fife. It was not identified in the report for closure, and on weekdays more than 20 trains ran from Dundee to St Andrews alone. British Transport Hotels opened its only new hotel in the town, on the site of the original station, and all looked well for this busy route. Nevertheless, closure of this well-used section of line was proposed by BR – and was met with considerable anger in St Andrews. A campaign was mounted, but to no avail; passenger services between Leven and St Andrews were withdrawn in September 1965, and those between St Andrews and Leuchars in January 1969. The Thornton Junction–Leven line, similarly, was not identified for closure in the Beeching report, yet it closed to passengers in October 1969. A section from Thornton Junction survived for coal to Methil power station. The power station was decommissioned

in 2000, but overgrown track still remained in 2010, when the power plant was demolished.

The main station at St Andrews was demolished, the site being now occupied by a car park, but a number of other station buildings remain on the coastal section. In particular, mention should be made of Strathivie station, where a railway carriage is used for accommodation, while Kirkland Yard, at Leven, is home to stock belonging to the Kingdom of Fife Railway Preservation Society. There has been continuous lobbying for reopening of the St Andrews–Leuchars and Thornton Junction–Leven sections. Surveys have shown that almost 80% of people in St Andrews support reopening, and there can be little doubt that, should the trains run again, they would be well patronised.

Below Class B1 4-6-0 No 61308 at the well-kept Cameron Bridge station with the 8.40am Saturdays-only Edinburgh–Crail train on 4 July 1964. A year later the flowerbeds were overgrown, but passenger services continued until October 1969. The rusting disused tracks to the now-closed Methil power station remained *in situ* in 2010 and plans to reopen the Thornton Junction–Leven section have been considered. *C. Thornburn*

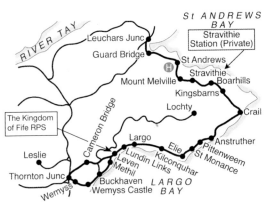

EXPRESS SERVICE GLASGOW and EAST FIFE DAILY (Except Sundays) THE FIFE COAST EXPRESS				
	p.m.			a.m.
Glasgow (Queen Street) lev.	4. 7	St. Andrews - lev.		7.14
Burntisland - arr.	5.14	Crail - - - ,,		7.36
Kirkcaldy - - ,,	5.29	Anstruther - ,,		7.44
Leven - - ,,	5.54	Elie - - - ,,		7.59
Elie - - - ,,	6.10	Leven - - ,,		8.14
Anstruther - ,,	6.21	Kirkcaldy - - ,,		8.37
Crail - - - ,,	6.30	Glasgow		
St. Andrews - ,,	6.53	(Queen Street) arr.		9.50

For other Services between Glasgow and St. Andrews, etc.—See Tables 95, 101, 102

Above 'Fife Coast Express' timetable for the summer of 1950.

Left Ex-NBR Class D30 4-4-0 No 62418 *The Pirate* at Largo on 22 April 1957, with the 2.30pm from Crail to Glasgow Queen Street; sister locomotive No 62468 *Glen Orchy* is in the loop with the 2.38pm Thornton Junction–Crail. The disused railway viaduct survives today as a prominent feature in the town. *W. Smith*

Below Elie station on 21 April 1954 with the 12.17pm Dundee–Edinburgh stopping train, headed by 'B1' No 61118. Note the camping coach on the right. *E. Patterson*

Above The 4.51pm Saturdays-only Thornton–Anstruther train, headed by 'B1' No 61133, pauses at a busy St Monance on 10 August 1963. Between 1875 and 1936 the station was known as St Monans. Today just the stone platform edge survives. *C. Thornburn*

Right Class B1 No 61146 leaving the remote Pittenweem station on 10 August 1963 with the 5.48pm Saturdays-only Anstruther–Thornton Junction. Apart from fishing, Pittenweem once had two coal mines and also produced salt by heating seawater. *C. Thornburn*

Above Class B1 No 61101 waits to be passed at the Anstruther bay platform, a former loop, with a Summer Saturdays-only special on 13 July 1963. The loop was replaced by one to the west of the station. At the height of the herring season the harbour at Anstruther would have once been packed with fishing boats. *C. Thornburn*

Below Crail station on 21 April 1954, with the 2.17pm Dundee–Edinburgh stopping train (left) passing the 2.39pm Thornton Junction–Crail stopper, hauled by B1 No 61118. The four intermediate stations between Crail and St Andrews were all closed in September 1930 by the LNER. *E. Patterson*

Facing page The driver of ex-LMS Compound 4-4-0 No 40924 hands in the single-line tablet on arrival at Crieff with a train from Perth. The line from Almond Valley Junction to Crieff closed to passengers in 1951, dating this view to c1950. *R. Stephen*

Left 'Black Five' 4-6-0 No 44925 waits to leave St Andrews with the Saturdays-only 4.8pm train to Glasgow on 24 August 1963. The northern (St Andrews–Leuchars Junction) section of the coastal route closed in January 1969. *C. Thornton*

Below Ex-NBR Class J37 0-6-0 No 64615 with a Leuchars Junction–St Andrews train crossing Guard Bridge over the River Eden, on 1 March 1958. The stone barrel footings of the girder bridge still survive. *W. Sellar*

13

Crieff and Comrie contraction

The 9-mile line from Crieff Junction to Crieff, like that between Leuchars and St Andrews, had Thomas Bouch as its engineer. He had promised opening of the line in September 1855, and staff were appointed with this date in mind.

However, arguments between Bouch and the contractor, as well as problems with a local landowner (who, upon being refused her own private station, denied the railway access to local water supplies), resulted in a deep well having to be built at Crieff station. This all caused delays, and the line eventually opened in March 1856.

An easterly 16¼-mile link between Crieff and Almond Valley Junction (1½ miles north of Perth) opened in January 1858. The 6-mile extension to Comrie opened in June 1893, by which time Crieff, a market town on the edge of the Highlands, had developed to become the second-largest town in

Perthshire. A substantial new through station, with 700ft (213m) platforms and glass canopies covering half their length, was constructed by the CR in conjunction with the extension to Comrie.

The Comrie–Balquhidder link opened as far as St Fillans in October 1901 and to Balquhidder, some 30 miles from Crieff Junction, by May 1905. This last section of line was built with mainly concrete bridges and viaducts. It ran through attractive countryside and was promoted as a tourist route, but it passed through a remote area and never really prospered.

In 1919 Crieff Junction was elegantly rebuilt and renamed Gleneagles, to reflect the importance

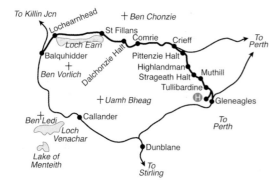

of the new hotel that was being built close by (and opened in 1924). The lines all became part of the LMS in 1923. At this time the original Gleneagles–Crieff route was still busy, seeing 12 passenger trains per day. The same could not be said of the Comrie–

Right Ex-CR Class 439 0-4-4T No 55208 at Crieff station, on 17 September 1949, before taking the Perth–Balquhidder train forward. Even by this time it was clear that the station had been built to an over-ambitious scale relative to the numbers of passengers carried. *H. Bowtell*

Below A general view of the vast Crieff station on 9 July 1956, with a DMU at the down platform on an experimental service between Gleneagles Junction, Crieff and Comrie. Even today the former station, with its centre third track, is fondly remembered locally in artists' sketches. *J. Dewar*

Balquhidder link, on which poor connections to a limited number of trains did little to encourage travellers, and this closed to passenger trains in October 1951. Thereafter occasional freight trains ran in connection with the Breadalbane hydro-electric scheme, and the track was not lifted until 1959. Passenger services over the direct line to Perth were also withdrawn in 1951, as a number of trains ran as part of a through Perth–Balquhidder service.

The Beeching report specifically highlighted the remaining Gleneagles–Comrie branch. It recorded that 10 DMUs a day carried an average of five passengers at any one time, with the result that fares covered only one tenth of the costs of the branch. Accordingly the Gleneagles–Comrie service was withdrawn in July 1964, although through freight to Crieff, via the Perth line, continued until September 1967.

Left The 4.48pm Gleneagles–Crieff railbus arriving at Crieff station, on 18 July 1961. These vehicles were the mainstay of the branch for a while before its closure. Note the driver peering out of the window; the railbuses did encounter some operational problems. Crieff station would be demolished in 1965. S. *Rickard*

Below English Electric diesel shunter No D3535 at Crieff goods yard with the 1.45pm return working of the 9.15am freight from Perth on 22 August 1966. Crieff had an important market and was the second-largest town in Perthshire, creating a busy railway goods yard. *L. Sandler*

Above Comrie station on 20 May 1961, with modernisation having come in the form of diesel railbus SC79978. The station had been the terminus of trains from Gleneagles since 1951, when the line to Balquhidder was closed to passenger traffic. After final closure of Comrie station in 1964 the site became part of a caravan park. *T. Williams*

Right Although the LMS as an organisation ceased in 1948 and rail freight to Crieff ended in 1967, when your author visited Crieff goods yard in September 1983 a building still marked 'LMS Goods Office' remained. The site has since been redeveloped. *Author*

Right St Fillans was an intermediate station on the Comrie–Balquhidder section of line. The beautiful surroundings attracted summer tourists, but this section of line was the first to close to passengers, in October 1951. The station and ex-CR signalbox still survive as part of a caravan site, the box being seen here in October 2011. *John Roddis*

BALQUHIDDER

Right The immaculately restored Lochearnhead station, seen in March 2009. The station was abandoned for 10 years until acquired by the Hertfordshire Scouts as a base for outdoor activities. It was restored maintaining its original features and contains a small museum of memorabilia from its railway past. *John Roddis*

Left At Gleneagles the ex-railway hotel remains open, as does the elegant Edwardian junction station, the latter giving an insight as to how opulent Crieff station would have once been. This October 2011 photograph at Gleneagles station was taken in the direction of the former Crieff lines and provides a good view of the overgrown footbridge that once provided access to the booking office. *Author*

14

An ABC of Scottish branches

Alva was served by a 3½-mile branch from Cambus, opened in June 1863. There were once nine woollen mills at Alva, and workers' cottages were built to a gridiron plan. The mills used water from the Ochil Hills, and textiles constituted an important freight on the branch. Mills were also found at the sole intermediate station, Menstrie, along with yeast and furniture factories. Also generating traffic for the line were a distillery and a coal pit at Glenochil.

Passenger services were withdrawn in November 1954, and general freight ceased in March 1964. The branch was then cut back to the yeast factory at Menstrie, and molasses trains continued to use this section until 1993. A short section of track was still to be found at Menstrie in 2011, but the rest of the branch has been lifted, and some of the trackbed is now used as a cycleway. At Cambus, however, the rails have been renewed for the reopened railway to Alloa.

Beith Joint station was the terminus opened in June 1873 by the Glasgow, Barrhead & Kilmarnock Joint Railway. In 1953 it was renamed Beith Town by BR, to distinguish it from the Beith North station on the nearby ex-GSWR main line. Even though Beith North had closed to passengers in 1951 it remained open for freight traffic until October 1963. The 5-mile Lugton–Beith Town line closed to passengers in November 1962 and to general freight

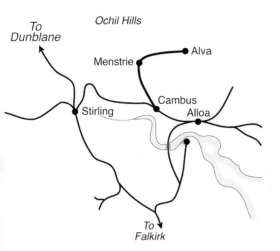

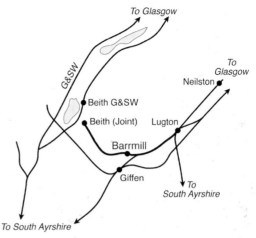

Facing page Alva station on 16 September 1950, with ex-NBR Class J36 0-6-0 No 65307 in charge of the 1.28pm train for Alloa. Passenger services ceased in November 1954, and freight in March 1964. The station house still survives. *H. Bowtell*

in October 1964. The Lugton–Barrmill section of the branch remained extant until the 1990s for traffic to the MoD site at Giffen, reached via a connection from the branch to the ex-CR line to Ardrossan. The connecting points at Lugton were removed in 2008, but some overgrown track remained in 2010.

Catrine was once a thriving mill town, and the branch was a late addition to the GSWR network, opening in March 1903 for freight and running some 3½ miles from Brackenhill Junction. Catrine–Mauchline passenger trains were introduced from

September of the following year. Services were suspended during 1917/18, and subsequently trains were operated for a time by a steam railmotor known locally as the 'Catrine Caur'. However, patronage was light, and in May 1943 the branch was closed to passengers by the LMS; freight survived longer, until July 1964. Little remains today, but the beautiful Ballochmyle Viaduct, with the largest and highest stone arch in Britain, is to be found on the nearby main line.

Dundee was the southern terminus of the Dundee & Newtyle Railway. This early line, built to a 4ft 6½in gauge and opened in December 1831, eventually ran to 16¾ miles. The first railway in the north of Scotland, it was also the first not to rely on coal as its most important source of revenue. The

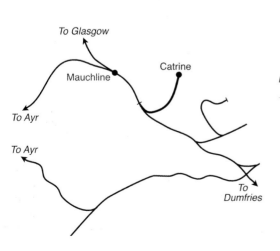

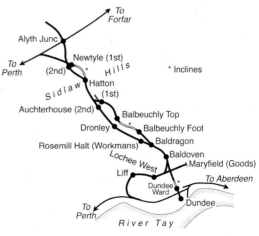

original line crossed the Sidlaw Hills by a series of three inclines worked by three stationary steam engines; elsewhere horses were employed, but in 1833 these were replaced by two locomotives. Originally intended for general goods traffic, the line was extended to Dundee docks and in February 1837 opened to passengers. In 1865 it was taken over by the CR. The inclines were eventually replaced by deviations with gentler gradients, and standard gauge was adopted. The railway retained its identity until the Grouping in 1923. Passenger services were withdrawn in January 1955, and by November 1967 the remaining southern section of this historic route was closed to freight.

Right A Class 20 diesel locomotive shunting at the Menstrie Glenochil yeast plant on 24 April 1981. The molasses tanker trains once ran to and from the James Watt Dock at Greenock. Menstrie became the terminus of the Cambus–Alva branch line in 1964, when freight was withdrawn from the Menstrie–Alva section. A short section of disused track still remained at the Menstrie plant in September 2011, but the remaining branch track had been removed.
D. Brittain-Catlin Brucefield

Below With snow on the Ochil Hills, the same Class 20 returns to Cambus Junction, having taken its tankers up to the works at Menstrie on 24 April 1981.
D. Brittain-Catlin Brucefield

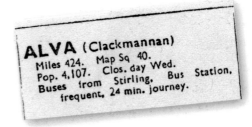

Above Alva ABC guide, 1930.

Above Alva ABC guide, 1956.

Above Beith Town station on 26 May 1956, with a Lugton train headed by ex-CR 0-4-4T No 55203. Known originally as the 'joint station' at Beith, it was formally renamed by BR in 1953 to distinguish it from the ex-GSWR goods facility at Beith North. *J. Robin*

Right Ex-CR 0-4-4T No 55203 seen between Barrmill and Lugton with the 12.47pm Beith–Lugton branch train on 7 July 1956. Although connections were provided at Lugton for Glasgow St Enoch it was suggested that if Beith trains were extended to Neilston, where frequent electric trains ran to Glasgow, the branch could have been saved from closure. A petition was raised, but BR refused to consider this proposal. *C. Dick*

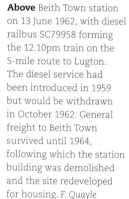

BEITH (Ayr). 406 miles. Fares, 83/8a. 50/3c; Return, double. From London as to Kilmarnock, thence 45 minutes, about 4 times daily. Pop. 6.343.

Above Beith ABC guide, 1930.

Right Beith ABC guide, 1956.

BEITH (Ayr)
Miles 405. Map Sq. 40.
Pop. 4,347. Clos. day Wed.
TOWN STATION.
From St. Pancras or Euston.
1st cl.—Single 95/6, Return 191/-.
3rd cl.—Single 63/8, Return 127/4.
Local trains from Kilmarnock (Week-days only), changing at Lugton, about 50 min. journey.
Buses from Glasgow, Clyde Street, or Waterloo Street, frequent, 62 min. journey.

Above Beith Town station on 13 June 1962, with diesel railbus SC79958 forming the 12.10pm train on the 5-mile route to Lugton. The diesel service had been introduced in 1959 but would be withdrawn in October 1962. General freight to Beith Town survived until 1964, following which the station building was demolished and the site redeveloped for housing. *F. Quayle*

Left Catrine station in April 1964, with 'Black Five' 4-6-0 No 45497 leaving with a freight train for Ayr. The line was one of the last to be built in Scotland, in 1903. A steam railmotor was used for a time, but passenger traffic was light, and the station closed to passengers in 1943. Freight survived longer, until 1964. The site has since been landscaped. *D. Cross*

Above BR Standard Class 5 4-6-0 No 73100 seen ¼ mile from Catrine with a goods train for Mauchline and Ayr in April 1964. Catrine itself was originally designed as a model village around one of the first cotton mills in Scotland. *D. Cross*

Left The Catrine–Ayr pick-up goods on 31 March 1964, headed by 'Crab' 2-6-0 No 42740. Note the letters 'L M S' still visible on the tender. Today much of the cutting at Catrine has been infilled and landscaped. *D. Cross*

Right Catrine ABC guide, 1930.

CATRINE (Ayr). 380 miles. Fares, 79/10a, 47/11c; Return, 159/8a, 95/10c. From St. Pancras as to Old Cumnock. To London about 4 times daily. Pop. 2,274.

Right A Dundee & Newtyle Railway bridge of distinctive design and with a keystone dated 1835. Beyond the bridge is a level crossing and gatekeeper's house, possibly locating this undated view near Alyth Junction. Although this bridge would appear to have been demolished, the original Newtyle station is still to be found nearby (see *Lost Lines: Scotland*). *Ian Allan Library*

Facing page Road, rail and sea transport all met at Aberdeen. Ex-GNSR Class Z5 0-4-2T No 68192 crosses the road from the harbour at Aberdeen on 22 May 1957. Even at this time heads would turn at the sight of a freight train crossing a road of granite sets in the 'Granite City'. *John Spencer Gilks*

Above Originally the line was built for general freight traffic such as agricultural produce, coal and stone from local quarries. The daily mixed goods continued this tradition, being seen here trundling along the one-time Dundee & Newtyle Railway behind ex-LNER Class J39 0-6-0 No 64950. The photograph was taken in 1957. *T. Mahoney*

Above Map of the railway near Newtyle in 1926, showing the snaking deviation required to gain height when the incline, on the original line south of Newtyle, was taken out of use. *Crown copyright*

Below Ex-NBR Class J37 0-6-0 No 64620 climbs from Ninewells Junction with the 10.30am Dundee–Maryfield coal train on 13 April 1966. Passenger services ceased in January 1955, and all remaining freight in November 1967. *P. Riley*

15

Aberdeen Harbour

The harbour at Aberdeen was long established, and the port authorities were apprehensive of the effect the railways would have on its trade. They wanted any lines to be laid away from the harbour, avoiding the centre of the city altogether, and accordingly the first station was built to the south of Aberdeen, at Ferryhill.

This opened in 1850 but closed in 1854 when agreement was reached for the line to be extended to Guild Street in the city centre and alongside the harbour. The GNSR opened its line to Waterloo, northeast of the harbour, to freight in September 1855 and to passengers in April 1856.

The need to link the railways led to the first joint CR/GNSR station being opened in November 1867, enabling Guild Street station to become a goods depot. As it turned out, the railways encouraged greater use of the harbour, and the port became the busiest in the North of Scotland, with construction of the Albert Basin and other deepening and dock improvements being undertaken.

The CR goods depot at Guild Street was extended several times, and its vast extent was indicative of the sheer volume of goods that was handled. The GNSR provided an adjoining goods yard, called Deeside. Freight tramways linked all the goods depots by a series of street lines and provided quayside sidings on either side of the main harbour and to the quayside fish market.

Aberdeen Harbour was the focus for coastal vessels, and cargoes of wood, granite and livestock were established. Yet fresh fish became particularly important because the quality was high, as trawlers returning from the fishing grounds had a shorter trip to Aberdeen than to English ports. As a consequence steam trawlers using Aberdeen Harbour increased from about 40 in the 1890s to 178 vessels in 1904. The increase in catches resulted in a similar increase in the quantities of fish that were transported by rail. Fish boxes were dispatched on passenger trains, fish wagons were attached to passenger trains and entire express fish trains were run. The NBR ran a daily overnight fish train to London, arriving at King's Cross in the early hours. By the 1890s the CR was also offering a daily service. Fish trains were also provided to Manchester, Birmingham and other cities. The importance of perishable fish not being delayed was paramount, and on occasions fish trains would be dispatched ahead of passenger expresses. The railways also began to use ice to keep the fish fresher, and the fish trains underpinned the success of Aberdeen's fishing industry.

World War 1 saw the harbour being heavily used to service the Grand Fleet, based at Scapa Flow. Conversely World War 2 caused considerable damage to the area and also prevented the fishing fleet from being used to any great extent. On the plus side, by the time fishing resumed postwar, fish

stocks had been replenished, and catches were huge. Between 1949 and 1961 BR provided a new fleet of distinctive white insulated fish vans for the dedicated Aberdeen–London services, but by this time fish stocks were falling, and Aberdeen declined as a fishing port. Nevertheless fish vans from Peterhead and Fraserburgh were added to Aberdeen trains, and even in 1963 about 75 fish vans were still departing daily from Aberdeen.

In 1964 BR proposed to cut the fish trains from Aberdeen to two trains. As late as 1966 a daily Aberdeen–London fish train was still running and was well patronised. However, as a result of increases in rates and decreases in the average speed of the train (down from 75mph to 45mph) which upset long-standing customers the remaining fish train from Aberdeen to London King's Cross ceased running in January 1976.

The harbour lines were used for a number of enthusiast trips, the last such being in 1972 when a locomotive from the Aberdeen Gasworks, which was connected to the harbour network, was used. Major quay restoration work in the late 1980s saw the removal of the tracks on the north side of the harbour, but sections of disused quayside track could still be found on the south side of Victoria Dock in 2012. Guild Street depot is now closed, but rail-borne freight is still handled at Waterloo.

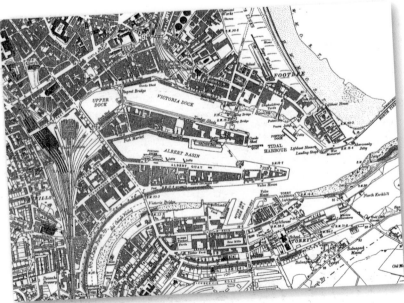

Left Map of Aberdeen Harbour in 1930. The North Pier was built partly by Thomas Telford. Victoria Dock was completed in 1848 and so named following a visit by Queen Victoria. *Crown copyright*

Left Four locomotives were built by Manning, Wardle & Co for the GNSR in 1915 for duties at Aberdeen Harbour, after the harbour authorities had finally agreed to allow steam to replace horses for haulage. This close-up view of Class Z4 0-4-2T No 68190 in BR livery at Waterloo goods was recorded shortly before the locomotive's withdrawal in 1960. The buildings and track seen here are no more, but freight traffic survives. *J. Emslie*

Right Class Z5 0-4-2T No 68193 shunting at Aberdeen Harbour on 5 July 1950. The two classes were very similar, but the 'Z4s' had 3ft 6in wheels and were lighter, while the 'Z5s' had larger (4ft) wheels and originally had to run with half empty tanks to reduce their weight. Both classes had short wheelbases to negotiate the tight quayside curves and were based at Kittybrewster. No 68193 would be the first locomotive withdrawn, in 1956. *C. McCallum*

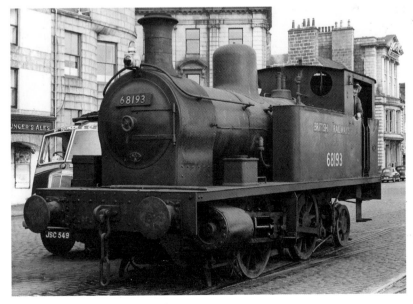

Left Class Z5 No 68193 at Aberdeen Harbour on 23 September 1955. The 'Z' classification was first introduced by the LNER. It is of note that BR livery was applied differently to the side tanks of each locomotive. *P. Wells*

Facing page Track removal under way at Aboyne station in May 1970, this being the view towards Ballater. The granite station was built to a baronial design and handsomely decorated with turrets and spires. Although it has since lost its platform canopies, it survives as a listed building. *A. Muckley*

Left Class Z4 No 68191 at Aberdeen in July 1955. The numbering of the harbour locomotives was interesting. This GNSR locomotive was originally No 117 but was renumbered 44 by the GNSR. The LNER added 6,800 to all GNSR locomotives, and as such this became No 6844, but then the LNER renumbered it as 8191 in 1943; BR added 60,000, hence it was finally withdrawn as No 68191, in 1959. *J. Gibbons*

Left One of the BR Blue Spot fish vans, with a distinctive blue spot painted on a white background on each side, photographed on 14 January 1958. The vehicle was fitted with roller bearings, for sustained high-speed running. The wording on the right makes clear that it was to work only between Aberdeen and King's Cross. *BR*

Below Class 08 diesel shunter No 3558 shunts a train of BR-built fish vans at Aberdeen on 7 November 1973. Some of the sidings on the right extended as far as the harbour, while on the far left can be seen the huge Guild Street freight depot. All have since been removed as part of the redevelopment of this city centre site. *B. Morrison*

16

Royal Deeside revisited

As the railway edged its way up Deeside, reaching Ballater, some 43 miles from Aberdeen, in October 1866, the Aboyne & Braemar Railway – as its name suggests – had every intention of taking the railway line to Braemar. Consequently Ballater was designed as a through station, while to the west a road overbridge was built in anticipation of extending the line to Braemar.

In 1866 a Colonel Farquharson agreed to extend the line to enable timber to be transported from his estate, and well-constructed line, with bridges, was laid on a steadily rising grade on the northern bank of the River Dee, continuing 1½ miles northwest from Ballater, as far as the abutments of the proposed railway bridge over the River Gairn, at the aptly named Bridge of Gairn. However, the railway was still some 15 miles short of its intended objective of Braemar.

It was intimated that the new line was a mere tramway as far as Bridge of Gairn, where it was to connect with a further tramway to transport logs from Ballochbuie Forest. The unassuming description was intended not to alarm Queen Victoria, for whom Balmoral Castle had been purchased by her late husband, Prince Albert, as a remote retreat, but the line was more than just a goods tramway. The route beyond Ballater was built to main-line standards, and the ultimate intention was doubtless to extend passenger services to Braemar, with an intermediate station at Crathie, close to Balmoral. Victoria was clearly 'not amused' by the prospect of hordes of

day-trippers arriving by train and now purchased Ballochbuie Forest, ostensibly to prevent its exploitation. Consequently the need for a 'tramway' to convey timber from the forest was no more, but Victoria's acquisition of the land equally frustrated the railway's plans to build over it.

Thwarted in its strategy to reach Braemar, in 1897 the railway unveiled plans for the line to be formally opened as far as Bridge of Gairn, and a hotel constructed, but these also found no favour with the royal household. The GNSR, which had taken over the Aboyne & Braemar Railway in 1876, was anxious not to offend the Queen, and, once it was realised that the railway was never going to reach Braemar during her lifetime, the track beyond Ballater was lifted, the official explanation being that the line was simply not required. The power of Queen Victoria should not be underestimated; even the Royal waiting room at Ballater was built to designs approved by her, and it would have been a brave railway company that attempted to build across her estate without her blessing.

Once Victoria was dead the idea was soon revived, but by this time the cost of providing a railway to the small village of Braemar was considered disproportionate. Even plans to use the easy grades of the Ballater–Bridge of Gairn trackbed as a road (for use by motor buses) were abandoned on grounds of cost in 1904. Nevertheless, a bus service linking Ballater with Braemar was introduced by the GNSR in the same year. At Braemar a booking office

displaying a huge GNSR sign and complete with railway uniformed staff was opened. Both Balmoral (in particular) and Braemar were also repeatedly shown as destinations on Scottish railway maps.

By the latter half of the 20th century the power of the monarchy was much diminished, and BR had no qualms about closing the Aberdeen–Ballater line. Despite strong opposition locally the attractive route closed to passengers in February 1966, the last Royal Train having departed Ballater in October of the previous year. Since final closure of the line to freight, in July 1966, and after a period of dereliction, the station at Ballater has been restored, and visitors can now view Queen Victoria's waiting room and other Royal Train memorabilia. Part of the line has been also been preserved as the Royal Deeside Railway, near Crathes Castle, while the extension beyond Ballater, together with other sections of former trackbed, now form the basis of footpaths.

Above Aboyne station in June 2009. The station seen here was built after opening of the line and dates from 1896. A plaque on the station records that Queen Victoria travelled via Aboyne in the period 1860-7 *en route* to Balmoral, before the line was extended to Ballater. *Author*

Above A railcar from Ballater draws into Dinnet station in August 1965. At one time GNSR charabancs connected with trains here; the summer excursions were marketed as Two or Three Rivers Tours and offered trips to the Dee, Don and Spey. *A. Muckley*

Right Cambus o' May opened in 1875, almost a decade after the railway to Ballater itself (opened in 1866). Before services ceased just one train a day, in each direction, stopped at what had latterly become a halt. This was the view east, just before track-lifting in May 1970. The line had closed in July 1966. *A. Muckley*

Below The platform edge at Dinnet in June 2009; it was on this platform that the signalbox would have been located. The main station building survives as an estate office. *Author*

Left The LNER provided camping coaches at the picturesque Cambus o' May, beside the River Dee, while gunpowder was once delivered to a nearby quarry. This attractive view of the halt was recorded in June 2009. A line proposed from Nethy Bridge was never built. *Author*

Above An unusual locomotive for this ex-GNSR line was ex-NBR Class D34 4-4-0 No 62479 *Glen Shiel*, pictured at Ballater on an Aberdeen-bound train in July 1953. The train comprises a rake of ex-LNER Gresley teak coaches painted in BR livery of carmine and cream. *Ian Allan Library*

Right Tourism was always an important part of the line's revenue. Today Ballater station has been restored and is now a tourist office and exhibition centre. The royal waiting rooms have been refurbished, and this replica of an 1869 royal coach could be found at the platform in June 2009. *Author's collection*

Above The road frontage of Ballater station in June 2009, restored as the Old Royal Station. The station was rebuilt in 1886, the much-improved facilities having been approved by Queen Victoria, who last used it in November 1900. Over the years it has been used by a host of royalty and dignitaries from all over the world. *Author*

Below Westward beyond Ballater, Royal Deeside and the majestic Grampian Mountains were a favourite haunt of Queen Victoria. Beyond Ballater and on towards Bridge of Gairn the railway trackbed forms an attractive walkway; 'The Old Line', as it is known in Ballater, is seen here above the River Dee in June 2009. *Author*

Table 110	Ballater and Braemar
(Motor Omnibus Service operated by Messrs. W. Alexander & Sons Ltd.)	
WEEKDAYS ONLY	
Ballater to Braemar—10·0 a.m; 12·15, 2·15, 4·15, 7·15, 9·15 p.m	
Braemar to Ballater—8·15, 11·15 a.m; 1·45, 4·15, 6·15, 8·15 p.m	

Above Ballater–Braemar bus services, 1950.

Below Part of a map of the line, produced by the North Eastern Railway and showing Balmoral as the key (but unconnected) railway destination. The ornamental barrow and spade used to cut the first sod of the extension of the line from Aboyne to Ballater, on 7 September 1865, are preserved at Balmoral Castle. *Author*

17

The Buchan branches

The line to Peterhead and Fraserburgh ran north from Dyce some 24¾ miles to a junction at Maud. From here a 13-mile line, opened in July 1862, ran east as far as Peterhead, while a 15-mile line, opened in April 1865, continued north to Fraserburgh. Further development of the network included the 15½-mile branch from Ellon to Boddam, opened in August 1896, and the 5-mile Fraserburgh–St Combs light railway, opened in July 1903. All these lines were eventually operated by the GNSR, that to St Combs being its only light railway.

Fish was the principal goods traffic. A branch line served the harbour at Peterhead, and here, as at Fraserburgh, the port was extended and improved to accommodate the ever-increasing number of steam trawlers. At one time three fish trains a day departed from Peterhead and two from Fraserburgh, although the third train from Peterhead combined with the Fraserburgh service at Maud Junction. At Aberdeen the fish vans would join dedicated fish trains destined for London and other major cities. While fresh herring was the main fish traffic, whale oil was once conveyed to Dundee, and tinned fish, fish curing and fishmeal all provided freight for the railway.

Tourism also developed, and on the Boddam branch a large hotel opened at Cruden Bay in March 1899. Owned by the GNSR, this was ahead of its

Facing page A busy Fraserburgh station in August 1965, with North British Type 2 diesel No D6123 heading one of the few and mostly all-station services to Aberdeen. The approximately 2hr timing for the 47¼ miles to Aberdeen in 1965 was hardly any quicker than when the line opened and indeed was appreciably slower than some of the 1hr 40min timings of 1910. The stone-built two-road locomotive shed seen in the distance is the only railway building to remain extant. *A. Muckley*

time and boasted electric lights and lifts. An 18-hole golf course was also provided. The hotel was largely dependent on passengers arriving by train, and an electric tramway led from the station to the hotel. Despite this the branch was never a financial success, and passenger services were withdrawn by the LNER in November 1932, further reducing the already dwindling numbers of guests arriving, for the short summer season, at the Cruden Bay Hotel. The latter was requisitioned by the Army during World War 2, and the tramway closed in 1940. The branch finally closed to freight in November 1945, but a buyer could not be found for the hotel, which was duly demolished.

The line from Aberdeen to Peterhead, via Maud Junction, was longer than the road link, and the limited number of trains for the most part stopped at most stations. Despite this connections were generally poor, and there was a failure to provide a worthwhile commuter service to and from Aberdeen. Diesel locomotives and multiple-units were introduced by BR, but otherwise there was little attempt at modernising the line or speeding up the service. On the freight side, the declining herring shoals also dictated a reducing number of fish trains.

Dr Beeching identified all the remaining Buchan lines for closure to passengers. In respect of the Maud Junction–Peterhead and Fraserburgh–St Combs sections this was effected in May 1965, while the Dyce–Fraserburgh service was withdrawn in October of that year. Beeching also targeted the remaining fish traffic, although valiant efforts were made to forward fish by Freightliner services from Fraserburgh. There remained rail freight in fertiliser, as well as materials for constructing pipelines for the growing North Sea oil and gas industry. Nevertheless freight traffic to Peterhead ceased in September 1970, and that to Fraserburgh in October 1979.

The closure of the Buchan lines was not without controversy, leaving busy Fraserburgh and Peterhead, the latter the area's largest town, without rail transport and contributing to road congestion. The stations at Peterhead and Fraserburgh have been demolished, but buildings at Maud Junction survive and include a small railway museum. Much of the trackbed now forms the basis of the Formartine & Buchan Way, a long-distance cycle path.

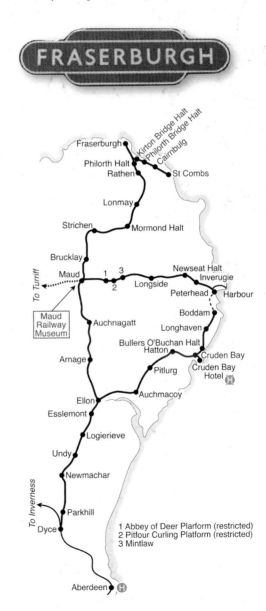

Right Class F4 2-4-2T
No 67151 heads a train
of vintage six-wheeled
coaches at St Combs in
August 1950. The ex-GER
locomotive was transferred
to the branch by the LNER.
Note the cow-catchers that
were provided for running
on this unfenced light
railway. *C. Kerr*

Above A DMU at St Combs
with the 3.55pm to Fraserburgh
on 19 April 1963. The platform
buildings were demolished
before closure, and an old goods
van sufficed as the facilities.
The pay-train services were well
used, as there was no competing
bus service, and closure was
highly controversial. *L. Sandler*

Right English Electric Type 1
No D8031 with the 10.15am Class
C Fraserburgh–Aberdeen fish
express near Rathen, on 13 July
1960. Various fish products, fresh
herring in particular, provided
most freight for the line. *J. Emslie*

Left Headed by an unidentified BRCW Type 2 diesel, the midday Fraserburgh–Aberdeen fish train passes the remote Rathen Halt in August 1965. This former station, reduced to a halt in 1926, had closed to goods traffic in 1960 and would close altogether in October 1965. *A. Muckley*

Below Headed by NBL Type 2 No D6123, an Aberdeen–Fraserburgh train pauses at Mormond Halt, where it called by request on Saturdays only. The photograph was taken in August 1965. The former station had become an unstaffed halt in 1939, goods facilities being withdrawn the following year. All services ceased in October 1965. *A. Muckley*

Above A view of the station buildings at Maud Junction, recorded on 15 June 1956. Maud Junction, originally named Brucklay Junction, developed to become a busy rural station and once boasted a dining room. The Peterhead platforms are seen here. *J. Halliday*

Right The Peterhead platforms at Maud Junction, pictured in February 1972. A new village developed around the junction at Maud, located in the rolling and bare Buchan countryside. Agricultural traffic – cattle in particular – was once important. Today a railway museum is located in one of the remaining station buildings. *A. Muckley*

Right When it assumed control in 1948 BR put an end to goods traffic on the short Peterhead harbour branch, although the station continued to handle freight until 1970. Peterhead station is seen here on 5 September 1970, with the GNSR Association's special last train hauled by Class 26 No D5307. In the long term, and with continued growth of the town, a return of the railway to Peterhead has not been entirely discounted. *D. Cross*

Left The erstwhile GNSR network suffered more than its fair share of closures. A derelict Peterhead station, looking east, after track-lifting in February 1972. Today the station site is occupied by a school, while the Formartine & Buchan Way uses much of the old trackbed. *A. Muckley*

Right Ellon–Cruden Bay timetable, April 1910.

Below Map of the tramway serving the Cruden Bay Hotel in 1901. *Crown copyright*

ELLON, CRUDEN BAY, and BODDAM.—Great North of Scotland.

Miles.	Down.	mrn	mrn	aft	aft	aft		Miles.	Up.	mrn		aft	aft		aft
	Week Days.								**Week Days.**						
	Ellon ......dep.	8 55	1025	1 40	5 20	8 0			Boddam ....dep.	7 40		1250	3 55		7 15
3¼	Auchmacoy....	9 5	1032	1 47	5 30	8 7		2	Longhaven §....	7 45		1255	4 0		7 20
5¼	Pitlurg	9 7	1037	1 52	5 35	8 12		5¼	Cruden Bay	7 53	9 40	1 3	4 8		7 23
8¼	Hatton	9 13	1043	1 58	5 41	8 18		7¼	Hatton	7 58	9 40	1 8	4 13		7 33
10¼	Cruden Bay § ..	9c26	1049	2 4	5 47	8 24		10	Pitlurg	8 4	9 59	1 14	4 19		7 39
13¼	Longhaven		1057	2 12	5 55	8 32		13¼	Auchmacoy....	8 10	10 6	1 20	4 25		7 45
15¼	Boddam .....arr.	9c30	11 2	2 17	6 0	8 37		15¼	Ellon 890....arr.	8 17	1015	1 27	4 32		7 52

§ Except Mondays.   § Bullers o'Buchan Platform between Cruden Bay and Longhaven.—All Trains will stop when a request by Passengers is made to the Guard at Cruden Bay or Longhaven, or when Passengers are upon the Platform to take up.

Above The attractive stone-built Inverugie station viewed in the direction of Peterhead in February 1972. The station closed to goods in 1960 and to passengers in 1965. A new building now occupies the site, and only a part of the platform remains. *A. Muckley*

Facing page Macduff station, with a BR Blue Spot fish van on the left. The station seen here opened in 1872 and closed in 1961, the year this photograph was taken. A stone building with an overall roof was provided to shelter passengers at this bleak coastal location, yet the station was not well sited for either the town or the harbour. The stone trainshed still survived in 2012. *D. Lawrence*

Above A view of Cruden Bay station, showing the ornamental masts for the 500V electric trams. The Cruden Bay Hotel's luggage & laundry van can also be seen on the narrow-gauge (3ft 6½in) track. The photograph is most likely to have been taken after passenger services were withdrawn in 1932 but before the trams were taken out of service in December 1940. The hotel's roofline can just be discerned on the horizon on the extreme right. *courtesy Grampian Transport Museum*

Middle The view north at Ellon Junction station in February 1972, including the disused Boddam-branch platform. Golfers heading for the course at Cruden Bay changed trains here, until passenger services were withdrawn in 1932. Little trace of the station can be found today. *A. Muckley*

Right Two trams were provided for the hotel service, and both tram bodies survived in a form that enabled one tram to be created for preservation, as seen here at the Grampian Transport Museum at Alford. Prior to closure of the line (in 1940) the trams, which provided the most northerly electric passenger service in Britain, had 'LNER' emblazoned on their sides. *courtesy Grampian Transport Museum*

18

Macduff mystery

The Banff, Macduff & Turriff Junction Railway built the first section of the 29¾-mile Inveramsay–Macduff branch, reaching Turriff in September 1857. The Banff, Macduff & Turriff Extension Railway then extended the line to a temporary terminus, at Gellymill (about a mile south of Macduff, but known as Banff & Macduff), opened in June 1860.

Because of the poor finances the line was not well built. Wooden fences rotted within the first year, and livestock was hit by trains. There were broken rails and more than 600 broken chairs; embankments were subject to subsidence, and cuttings were too narrow. The railway blamed the contractor, who blamed late payments by the railway. The companies involved with the line to Macduff struggled financially and were absorbed by the GNSR in 1866.

The final section was completed by the GNSR in July 1872, from the temporary terminus to a new stone-built facility at Macduff, with two platforms and an overall roof. A further station was opened on the extension at Banff Bridge. The new station at Macduff was high above the town, and although a tramway to the harbour was considered, the steep gradients involved made this impractical.

Examination of a map of the GNSR network reveals two straggling lines to the sea ports of Banff and Macduff, on opposite sides of the River Deveron. A road bridge linking the two had been constructed in the 18th century, and it seems curious that they

Inveramsay, Turriff and Macduff			Table 112
WEEKDAYS ONLY			

Mls		a.m.		p.m	p.m		Ex Sats / Sats only p.m p.m			a.m.		Sats only a.m	p.m	p.m	p.m	
..	Aberdeen .. .. lev.	8 30	..	2 35	4 10	..	6 10	6 10	Macduff .. .. lev.	6 40	..	1025	1220	2 40	5 10	..
..	Inveramsay .. lev.	9 12	..	3 20	4 58	..	7 27	7 2	Banff Bridge	6 43	..	1028	1223	2 43	5 13	..
3½	Wartle	9 19	..	..	5 5	..	7 9	7 9	King Edward	6 54	..	..	..	2 54	..	..
7½	Rothienorman ..	9 27	..	3 39	5 13	..	7 17	7 17	Turriff	7 11	..	1049	1247	3 10	5 37	..
10½	Fyvie	9 34	..	..	5 20	..	..	7 24	Auchterless	7 19	..	..	1255	3 18	..	..
14	Auchterless ..	9 41	..	..	5 27	..	..	7 31	Fyvie	7 28	..	11 3½	3 3	3 26	..	..
17¾	Turriff	9 50	..	3 58	5 38	..	7 35	7 39	Rothienorman	7 41	..	1111	1 2½	3 36	5 58	..
24½	King Edward ..	10 2	..	..	5 50	..			Wartle	7 48	..	..	1 19	3 43	6 5	..
29¼	Banff Bridge.. ..	1011	..	4 17	5 59	..	7 54	7 58	Inveramsay .. .. arr.	..	..	..	1 25	3 49	6 11	..
29¾	Macduff .. .. arr.	1014	..	4 20	6 2	..	7 57	8 1	Aberdeen .. .. .. arr.	8 44	..	1211	2 25	4 44	6 57	..

Left Timetable for the Macduff branch in the summer of 1950.

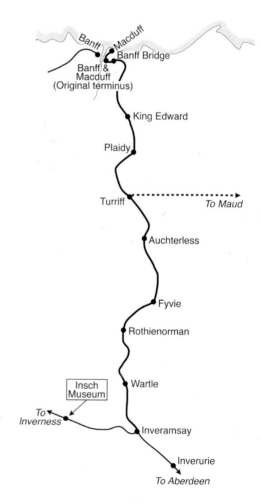

were not also linked by a railway bridge. However, it remains the case that none was ever built, so travelling by rail between the two ports would have involved a circuitous journey of some 75 miles.

A clue to the mystery lies in the fact that the two rival companies building separate lines to Banff and to Macduff reached their stated objectives, on either side of the river, within a year of each other. This having been achieved, they sought to exploit their respective coastal fishing ports but at the same time serve their different hinterlands. Each company was in a poor financial state, and the cost of a railway bridge to connect the two ports, for what would have been limited rail traffic, was not a priority. Furthermore, the local topography and existing development in and around Banff would have made any link problematical.

In any event it was originally anticipated that the Macduff line would attract trade from Banff, on the opposite side of the river. The railway offered commissions to traders who brought goods the short distance over the road bridge from Banff to their original station, called Banff & Macduff, but this did not attract much business from Banff.

Once the GNSR took over all the lines, both settlements and their ports were served by the same railway and had good links to Aberdeen, a key destination for much of the freight. Consequently, even assuming finance was available, there would have been little incentive to provide a direct line between two ports. However, in 1929 a bus service was operated between the two ports using the road bridge.

The fact that the lengthy branches competed with each other to serve relatively small towns led to their early demise. Passenger services to and from Macduff were withdrawn in October 1951, Banff thereafter being the nearest passenger station – until it also

closed, in 1964. Freight traffic between Turriff and Macduff ceased in August 1961, while the remaining Turriff–Inveramsay section of the branch closed in January 1966. The line was not heavily constructed, but several isolated remains are still to be found.

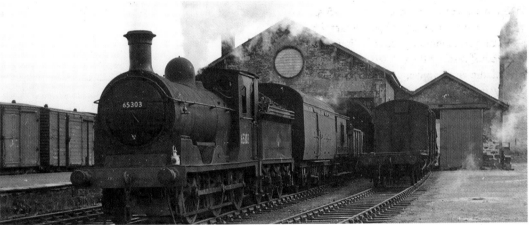

Top King Edward station viewed from the back of a southbound goods train on 1 June 1959. Although the line here was only ever single-track, the bridge seen on the right was built to accommodate a possible passing loop. The wooden station building survived, in a ramshackle state, in 2012. *John Spencer Gilks*

Above Ex-NBR Class J36 0-6-0 No 65303 prepares to leave Macduff with a mixed goods on 1 June 1959. Goods traffic to Macduff outlasted the passenger service by 10 years, finally ceasing in 1961, when freight was cut back to Turriff. *John Spencer Gilks*

Left Map of Macduff and surrounding area in 1900. *Crown copyright*

Facing page Calcots signalbox and station in December 1969, this being the view towards Elgin. Calcots was the first station on the coast route east from Elgin and was also the location of a passing loop on this single-track line. Today the site has reverted to agriculture. *A. Muckley*

Top Another view of No 65303 on 1 June 1959, this time at Turriff station, terminus of the branch before it was extended to Macduff. It was here also that traincrew changes were often effected. Today the station has given way to a caravan site, but some platform remains are to be found. *John Spencer Gilks*

Above The view south at Rothienorman on 1 June 1959. Until 1956 the station name had been rendered as two words – Rothie Norman. Although all the buildings have been demolished, a platform edge still survives, and part of the site is used as a car park. *John Spencer Gilks*

Left Inveramsay station yard, with the Macduff branch sidings on the right and the Inverness–Aberdeen main line on the left. The photograph, in common with most others in this chapter, was taken on 1 June 1959, the photographer having been granted a permit to travel along the branch after its closure to passengers. The station buildings at this site have since been demolished. *John Spencer Gilks*

19

Mouldering on the Moray coast

The first railway to the Moray coast was the 5¾-mile Elgin–Lossiemouth route, opened in August 1852 to great celebrations. Iron-ore traffic from the Tomintoul area to the harbour at Lossiemouth never materialised, but whisky exports and fish once provided significant goods traffic for the branch. Later the LNER provided through passenger services to and from Edinburgh and, for a time, a sleeping-car service to and from London.

In July 1859 the Banff, Portsoy & Strathisla Railway opened a 10-mile line from Cairnie Junction, on the Aberdeen–Inverness main line, to Tillynaught, where it forked, 2¾ miles northward to Portsoy and 6 miles northeast to Banff. The 14-mile coastal section between Portsoy and Portgordon resulted in the railway changing its name to the Banffshire Railway. However, financial troubles, compounded by severe winter weather and flood damage, led the railway

into financial difficulties and an amalgamation in 1867 with the GNSR, which built the remaining lines and connections. These included a line striking east from the Lossiemouth branch some 9 miles to Garmouth, opened in April 1884. The 3¾-mile Garmouth–Portgordon section completed the GNSR coastal network, in April 1886, and provided a third possible route between Keith and Elgin.

The last section of the coastal line to be built

included the largest bridge in the area, across the Spey Estuary. The seven spans included a central arched lattice span of 350ft (106m), the largest span on any single line in Britain.

At Cullen the line was originally intended to pass through the grounds of Cullen House, but the owner flatly refused, and the railway was forced into an expensive diversion through the town of Cullen itself. This resulted in five viaducts, and Cullen became known as the 'railway-arch town'.

Whilst passenger traffic was mostly of a local nature there developed a busy holiday trade during the short summer season on the Moray coast, which was promoted as the 'Scottish Riviera'. Special trains were run from Glasgow and Edinburgh, to Cullen in particular. In 1923 control of the lines passed to the LNER, which also made an effort to promote the holiday trade in the area.

The coastal line once saw significant fish traffic, and harbour branches were built at Buckie, Portsoy and Banff. Herring was the main catch, and women working as fish-gutters were given special cheap tickets to take baskets of fish to inland towns. Fish wagons were attached to passenger trains, but at the height of the herring season dedicated fish trains also ran from Lossiemouth and other ports along the Moray coast.

In the 1960s the herring-fishing industry collapsed, and the number of holidaymakers began to decline. The Lossiemouth branch closed to passengers

in April 1964 and to freight in March 1966, while the Tillynaught–Banff section, with its three halts, closed to passengers in July 1964. The Elgin–Cairnie Junction/Banff sections closed completely in May 1968.

As the photographs in this chapter show, by the winter of 1969/70 the track had been lifted and the station buildings left to moulder away. Moreover, with the loss of the railway, many hotels and boarding houses ceased trading. The miniature West Buchan Railway used a mile of track near Banff station in 1984/5, after which the station was demolished, and the track removed. Several sections of trackbed are now used as footpaths and cycleways, while railway remains are still to be discovered along the disused coastal routes.

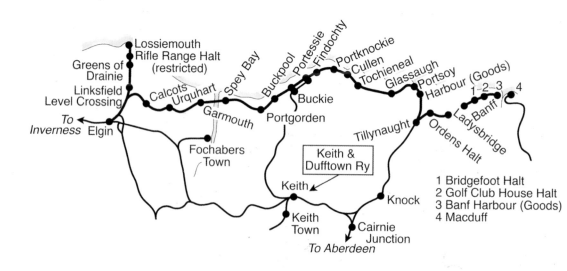

Facing page Urquhart station viewed in the direction of Garmouth in December 1969. At one time there was commuter traffic from the village to Elgin. Housing is to be found on the site today, but parts of the former trackbed are used as footpath. *A. Muckley*

Right Garmouth station was located on the western bank of the River Spey. This was the view east towards Spey Bay in February 1970. Note the corrosive effects of the sea air on the single enamelled platform sign. *A. Muckley*

Left Portgordon's single platform, viewed in the direction of Spey Bay in February 1970. The station buildings were among the few built on the south side of the line. Several of the station's fittings still remained at this time, including a seat, drinking fountain, lamp fittings and name board. After closure the station was used as a location in a film about World War 2 German spies. The buildings later became derelict and were eventually demolished, and the site is now used for recreation. *A. Muckley*

Right The exterior of Buckie station in February 1970. Piles of fish boxes are still to be seen, though the last train had run in May 1968. The station lingered, in an ever-deteriorating condition, and was finally demolished in 1980. Today little remains of the railway at this location. *A. Muckley*

Right Buckie's two platforms, viewed in the direction of Cullen in February 1970, the large goods shed being visible in the distance. Unusually for this route the station buildings were built of stone rather than wood, but this would not prevent demolition. *A. Muckley*

Below Findochty, with its scenic harbour and painted cottages, was once home to railway author George Behrend, who lived in Station Road. This photograph of the station platform, taken in the direction of Cullen in February 1970, shows the wooden station building, destined to be destroyed by fire in 1975. *A. Muckley*

Facing page top Cullen, on a sandy bay, was a popular tourist resort that was developed by the railway. In February 1970 the station remained intact aside from a lack of rails. Today the site is lost under housing development, but railway viaducts remain throughout the town and are used as footpaths and a cycleway. *A. Muckley*

Facing page bottom Portsoy was the last station on the coastal line before it turned inland towards Tillynaught Junction. Local marble provided some freight traffic for the railway, and until 1910 the harbour was served by a steeply graded branch from the main line. Viewed here in the direction of Cullen in February 1970 is the disused Portsoy station. The wooden station building, the second structure to be erected at this location, in 1884, has survived and is used today by the local scouts. *A. Muckley*

20

Spirits of the Spey

Speyside is associated with the production of some of Scotland's most famous single-malt whiskies. The railway assisted the growth of the whisky industry, and at one time most of the distilleries were served by rail. The distillery-related freight traffic comprised barley, coal and timber inwards and oak casks and cases of malt whisky outwards.

In August 1863 the Aviemore–Forres link provided the Highland Railway with a station at Boat of Garten. In August 1866 this also became the start of the 33½-mile GNSR Boat of Garten–Craigellachie line. Of interest was the embankment near Boat of Garten, which was shared by both railways, and where the HR's white ballast and the GNSR's pink ballast were still apparent years after the closure of both routes. *Lost Lines: Scotland* provides additional history of the Speyside line, while this chapter examines in greater detail those distilleries attached

to the route and which once generated much freight for the railway.

The snaking and expensive-to-build GNSR line followed the River Spey's southern bank for much of its route but crossed to the north bank between Ballindalloch and Carron, resulting in two fine bridges. This was whisky country, and consequently the GNSR's Boat of Garten–Craigellachie line was once a well-used section of railway for whisky-related freight. The railway brought the ingredients in and took the finished whisky out, and it is no coincidence

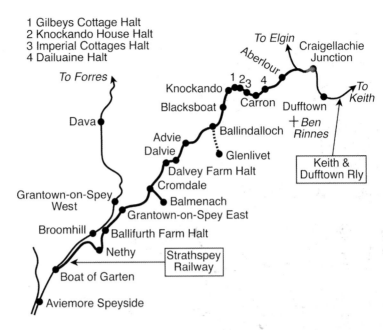

1 Gilbeys Cottage Halt
2 Knockando House Halt
3 Imperial Cottages Halt
4 Dailuaine Halt

Facing page New life in the form of a Park Royal railbus on an Aviemore–Craigellachie working pauses at Aberlour station in August 1965, but it would not save the line. The Station Bar in the background served a range of local malts. When the railway closed the name was changed to 'The Mash Tun', although the deeds stipulate that it must revert to 'Station Bar' should the railway ever reopen. The station buildings are used as a tea room and information centre. *A. Muckley*

that so many distilleries were either located beside the main line or connected to it by dedicated goods lines.

At Cromdale a 1½-mile whisky line led south to the distillery at Balmenach; the locomotive that worked the branch is now preserved on the Strathspey Railway. At Knockando, as it was known from 1905, a siding to the northwest of the main line led to the Tamdhu distillery. To the east of Carron a goods line ran to the southeast of the main line to serve the distillery at Dailuaine, and a halt of that name was opened on the main line in 1937. The

distillery locomotive also worked on the main line, taking wagons to and from Carron. To the west of Carron, Imperial Cottages Halt was opened as late as 1959, when railbuses were introduced on the route.

Below At the end of its life, but still well kept, ex-GNSR Class D40 4-4-0 No 62271 is seen at Blacksboat with a Boat of Garten–Craigellachie goods train in April 1953. Note the snowplough. At this time whole whisky trains were still run by BR. The kiln-like structure of the distillery in the background, known as a pagoda, was used for drying grain. *I. Smith*

Above English Electric Type 1 No D8031 calls at Carron station with the 2pm Craigellachie–Aviemore pick-up goods on 29 June 1966. Running on the wrong line, to facilitate shunting in the goods yard, the train consists mainly of wagons loaded with grain for use in whisky production. At this time the sizeable Imperial Distillery at Carron was an important customer for the railway; today, however, it is demolished. *J. Boyes*

Right Carron station, viewed in the direction of Aviemore in November 1970. The stone-built station building remained extant in 2012, but the signalbox has long since been demolished. The trackbed here now forms part of the Speyside Way, which links Aviemore with Buckpool, near Buckie. *A. Muckley*

Rail-connected distilleries were also to be found at Ballindalloch and Aberlour, while the Glenlivet distillery collected its barley and returned its whisky to Ballindalloch station. Originally dray horses were used and later lorries, as a proposed branch (of almost 6 miles) to the distillery was never built, on account of the steep gradients it would have entailed.

The valuable whisky-related rail traffic just ebbed away; indeed the last rail contracts are reputed to have been lost in part due to indifference by BR. The line between Boat of Garten and Craigellachie closed to passengers in October 1965 and to freight in November 1968, although the eastern stub to Aberlour remained open for whisky traffic until November 1971, closing just as there was a resurgence in sales of single malts.

Today much of the former trackbed forms part of the long-distance Speyside Way, and most of the station buildings remain. Aberlour is a visitor centre, Knockando now forms part of the adjoining Tamdhu distillery (and has been renamed as such), while Cromdale has been restored to its original condition. The railway has gone, but most of the distilleries remain, and at nearby Dufftown the Glenfiddich distillery still sees tourists arrive on the preserved Keith & Dufftown Railway, the 'Whisky Line'.

Above For travellers content with water, many stations were once equipped with drinking fountains, among them this cast-iron example, which survived at Knockando in November 1970. Such facilities have since been removed from most stations, but a working example can still be found at Bo'ness. *A. Muckley*

Above Speyside is associated with the production of Scotland's most famous single-malt whiskies. Here the Aviemore–Craigellachie railbus pauses at Dailuaine Halt, a request stop, in August 1965. The halt was added to the line by the LNER to serve the nearby distillery of that name, indicating the close relationship between the railway and the whisky industry. The halt's rotting wooden-edged platform and a nameboard were still to be found in 2011. *A. Muckley*

Below Knockando station, viewed in the direction of Aviemore. Known originally as Dalbeallie, it was renamed in 1905. In 1970 it was derelict, but by September 1977, when this photograph was taken, the station (along with the signalbox) was being maintained and had been renamed again as Tamdhu, ownership having passed to the adjoining Tamdhu distillery. *A. Muckley*

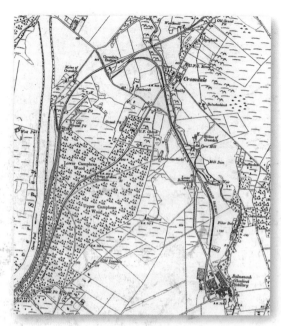

Above Map of the Balmenach Railway, serving the distillery of the same name, in 1905. *Crown copyright*

Below The 278ft (85m)-long lattice-girder bridge over the River Spey at Ballindalloch. The bridge plate records that it was built in 1863 by G. McFarlane of Dundee. The single-track bridge once conveyed whisky but is now part of the long-distance Speyside Way, which uses much of the old railway trackbed. *Author*

Facing page The extension to the Pier station was expensive to build, and crossing the River Oich at Fort Augustus involved construction of an imposing 300ft (91m) viaduct consisting of steel lattice girders supported by castellated concrete columns embellished with crosses. The Pier line closed to regular passengers in September 1906, after just three years of brief summer use. This view of the surviving concrete columns was recorded in June 2010. *Author*

Above In private ownership Cromdale station has been lovingly restored and is seen here in October 2011. Traces of the 1½-mile line that ran from the station yard to the Balmenach Distillery, which opened in 1897 and survived until 1968, can also be found in this area. The Barclay 'Pug' that worked the distillery line has been preserved on the nearby Strathspey Railway. *Author*

21

Abandoned at Fort Augustus

The Great Glen provided a natural communication route to Inverness, and there was considerable interest among railway companies in building a line along it. In addition there were a number of wealthy local individuals who wanted to bring the railway to the glen. They were also prepared to contribute funds, and this eventually led to the establishment of the independent Invergarry & Fort Augustus Railway.

The 24-mile Spean Bridge–Fort Augustus route was built along the glen as far as the shore of Loch Ness. Work began in 1897, but the line did not open until July 1903, due mainly to administrative errors by the railway's lacklustre management.

The railway was built to main-line standards, and land was bought for eventual double track. There were outsized stations, with optimistically large goods yards, even for the smallest of intermediate hamlets. Construction, involving a tunnel, swing-bridge and viaducts, proved so costly that there was no money left for rolling stock.

The West Highland Railway (WHR) offered to run the line, but the Highland Railway was alarmed that the ultimate destination of the railway was to be Inverness. Consequently the HR offered to work the line for 10 years and after a legal battle provided the best terms, in spite of the route being completely

FORT-AUGUSTUS and SPEAN BRIDGE.—Invergarry and Fort-Augustus.—North British.													
Mls		mrn		aft	aft		Mls			mrn		aft	aft
1	Fort-Augustus....dep.	8 30	Tues., Weds., and Fris.	2 30	Mons., Thurs., and Sats. 7 15	....	2¾	Spean Bridge ....dep.	1025	Tues., Weds. and Fris.	4 10	Mons., Thurs. and Sats. 9 15	....
4½	Aberchalder............	8 39		2 42	7 27	....	7½	Gairlochy	1033		4 22	9 27	....
9	Invergarry............	8 51		2 56	7 41	....	15	Invergloy Platform...	Sig.		Sig.	Sig.	....
16½	Invergloy Platform....	Sig.		Sig.	Sig.	....	19½	Invergarry	1059		4 59	10 4	....
21½	Gairlochy	9 17		3 33	8 18	....	23	Aberchalder............	1111		5 13	1018	....
24	Spean Bridge (above)a	9 25		3 45	8 30	....	24	Fort-Augustus....arr.	1120		5 25	1030	....

divorced from other HR lines. Once the HR's direct line from Aviemore to Inverness had been built the threat of a competing link via the Great Glen receded. In 1907 the NBR, which that year had absorbed the WHR, more sensibly took over running of the branch line to Fort Augustus.

Following the death of local benefactors, most notably Lord Burton (of Bass beer fame), receipts on the railway were revealed to be hopelessly inadequate. There was some timber freight, but the remote and heavily wooded area simply did not have sufficient population, or agricultural produce, to justify the line. September 1906 saw the last regular train use the Pier station at Fort Augustus, plans for a 'fast turbine-operated' Fort Augustus–Inverness railway ferry having been rejected. The sparse passenger service on the rest of the line was withdrawn in October 1911, with the intention of selling the assets for scrap.

This very early railway closure met with a storm of local protest and also aroused national concern, as the line had been open for just seven years. As a consequence services over the route were eventually reinstated, with support from the local council, in August 1913. The line became part of the LNER in 1923, and the attractive route was shown as a key part of the tourist network on its maps. Nevertheless, in its last months just a handful of passengers a day used the line, and it finally closed to passengers in December 1933.

Freight survived longer, and during World War 2 Fort Augustus was established as an emergency base for Inverness, in the event of the Highland main line being put out of action. A daily logging train was run, and a new platform added south of Fort Augustus to serve a Royal Naval Armaments Depot. After the war the line was used for one coal train a week, but this ran only until December 1946. A final single-coach special ran in March 1947, following which track-lifting was soon undertaken.

Above Timetable, April 1910.

The line was one of the last built in Scotland and used concrete for its bridges. Although it has been closed for more than half a century, remnants of many of these bridges and a tunnel can still be seen, while much of the route is clearly visible in the mountainous landscape. Indeed, to the walker following the route of the railway today it becomes clear that the views from this lost line would have been every bit as remarkable as its history.

Above In addition to bridges over mountain streams – and two small aqueducts over the line – numerous culverts and drains were required to prevent flooding of the railway in an area of heavy rainfall, and this all added to the cost of building the line. This concrete culvert and working drain could be found north of Aberchalder station in June 2010. *Author's collection*

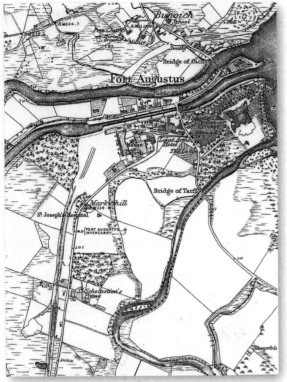

Left The railway arrives at Fort Augustus. A partly completed line appears on this map dating from 1900. *Crown copyright*

Below LNER map showing the Fort Augustus line as a main route. *Author's collection*

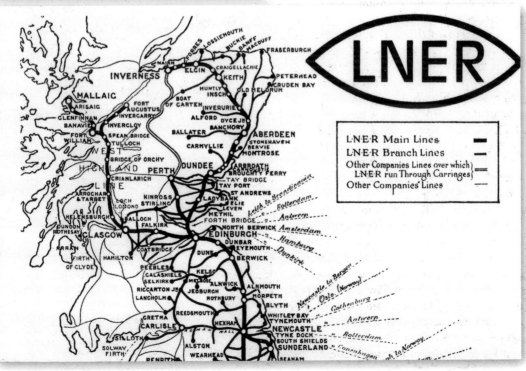

Right The skew-arched concrete bridge on the Pier branch at Fort Augustus. Built to a design that was characteristic of this line, with 'channelling' creating the effect of masonry, it was still in excellent condition when photographed in June 2010 and now spans a spur from the Caledonian Canal path. *Author*

Below The remains of the concrete pier at the southern tip of Loch Ness, photographed in June 2010. Passenger trains were originally scheduled to connect with the steamboat services of David MacBrayne. After closure of the Pier station to passengers, steamers ceased to call. Freight continued until closure of the station to all regular traffic in July 1924, although track remained for some time after this date. The gap in the centre of the pier allowed livestock to be driven down a ramp into the holds of ships. *Author's collection*

22

Highland and Island clearances

Although extremely picturesque, vast tracts of the remote Highlands and Islands are thinly populated and of little significant economic value. Yet several proposals for narrow-gauge passenger railways were promoted. Ultimately most schemes fell into abeyance, an exception being the Campbeltown & Machrihanish Railway, which is covered elsewhere in the 'Lost Lines' series.

Nevertheless, some narrow-gauge and miniature passenger lines were built on Scottish islands, to cater for summer tourists. The Rothesay & Ettrick Bay Light Railway opened in 1882, as a horse-worked tramway. By 1905 it had become a 5-mile-long, 3ft 6in-gauge double-track electrified tramway. The line was an early casualty and closed in September 1936. The miniature 7¼in-gauge Sanday Island Railway in the Orkneys was the most northerly passenger railway in the British Isles and after a brief existence closed in 2006. The 10¼in-gauge Mull Rail opened

in 1981 and provided a 1¼-mile island passenger line between Craignure and Torosay Castle; it closed in September 2011.

Elsewhere in the Highlands the standard-gauge branches of the HR were often short lines serving relatively small settlements located away from the main routes. They were operated economically, normally on the 'one engine in steam' principle and with mixed freight and passenger trains. Light railways were built in the far north to serve Lybster and Dornoch. Yet such is the sparseness of population that they were some of the first lines to lose their passenger services, and only one ex-HR branch – to Thurso – has survived.

Starting in the south, the delightfully scenic branch to Aberfeldy, 8¾ miles from Ballinluig, on the HR main line, opened in July 1865. The branch survived for just under a century, closing to all traffic in May 1965. Remains of the railway can still be found at the distillery at Aberfeldy, while Friockheim Viaduct, the largest of many structures on the heavily engineered branch, is now used as a footpath.

Although not built as a branch, the 26-mile Forres–Aviemore section of the erstwhile Highland main line was to become a secondary route when the new direct main line via Culloden was completed in 1898. The original single line remained in use until October 1965. Today the section from Aviemore to Broomhill is used by the preserved Strathspey Railway, which will ultimately extend its operations to Grantown-on-Spey West. Further north the Dava Way, a long-distance footpath, uses much of the former trackbed.

Previous page Isle of Mull Railway 2-6-2T Victoria, the largest tank engine built to 10¼in gauge, at Craignure. Pictured in September 1994, the train is awaiting arrival of the midday ferry from Oban. The island's railway closed in September 2011. *Ian Allan Library*

Below Aberfeldy station on 30 May 1959, with a train about to leave for Ballinluig behind ex-CR Class 2 0-4-4T No 55218. Few passenger coaches were required for most branch services, which typically were worked on the 'one engine in steam' principle. Mixed freight and passenger trains were also a feature of the HR branches. *W. Sellar*

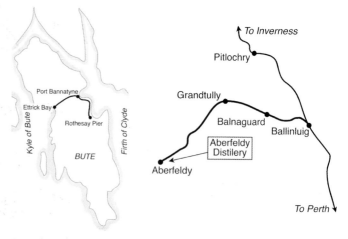

The 3-mile branch to Fochabers Town station opened in October 1893; at the same time the old Fochabers station, on the HR main line, was renamed Orbliston Junction. Even so, to avoid a costly bridge over the River Spey, the new terminus was still some way from the Georgian town on the east side of the river. The branch closed to passengers in September 1931, although freight survived until March 1966. The station buildings remain at both locations.

The 1½-mile branch to Fort George opened in July 1899, and for a time a ferry service was provided to Invergordon via Cromarty, on the Black Isle. The vast Fort George garrison provided military traffic for the line, including troop trains after its closure to regular passengers in April 1943, but the branch closed to all remaining traffic in August 1958.

Above Forres' partly demolished ex-HR signalbox and the trackbed of the line (now lifted) to Aviemore, over Dava Moor, feature in this scene, recorded in June 1970. The ex-HR Forres East signalbox remains today, the last survivor of three boxes that once controlled train movements at the junction station. *A. Muckley*

Left Little modernisation or investment was undertaken on the HR branches, but here BRCW Type 2 No D5336 is seen on arrival at an electrically lit Aberfeldy station with the 4.47pm from Ballinluig, on 18 April 1963. The station was demolished following closure, but a section of line and an industrial locomotive are to be found at the nearby distillery at Aberfeldy. *L. Sandler*

The 7½-mile branch to Burghead and Hopeman had opened throughout by October 1892. The line closed to passengers in September 1931. Fish and stone traffic at one time provided additional freight, but general freight to Hopeman ceased in December 1957, and to Burghead Harbour in November 1966. Block grain trains used the branch for a number of years in the 1970s and again in the late 1990s, and disused track from Alves to Roseisle, just south of Burghead station, was still to be found in 2012.

The nearby 5-mile Findhorn branch opened from Kinloss, on the main line, to the pier at the small sea port in April 1860. Passengers were conveyed, but it was built primarily to carry general cargo to and from ships using Findhorn's port. It was a very early financial failure and closed in January 1869, the track being lifted in 1873.

The 13¾-mile Keith–Portessie branch opened in August 1884, with the main aim of exploiting the fresh-fish traffic. The line closed in August 1915 as a World War 1 economy measure, and a 10-mile central section of track was removed for use elsewhere. The intention had been to reopen the branch after the war ended, but little progress was made in this regard. When the LMS took over it re-laid the track, but fish traffic had declined to such an extent that through working never resumed. A short stub from Keith to Aultmore survived for freight until October 1966.

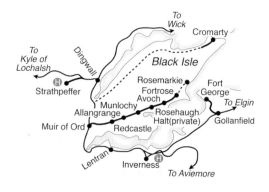

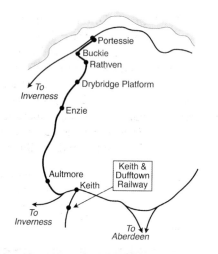

Below A new station was built at Burghead when the line was extended to Hopeman in 1892. Burghead's second station is seen here on 12 September 1958, with ex-CR 0-6-0 No 57620 in charge of a Forres–Elgin goods train ready to return to Alves. The line to Hopeman continued beyond the bridge. After a period of dereliction following closure, the attractive iron and wood listed station seen here was destroyed in an arson attack. *H. Botwell*

Right Class 37 No 37 183 waits at Alves for clearance off the Burghead branch with a Roseisle–Inverness grain trip working on 12 May 1984. Services had ceased by 2000, but disused rails from this point to the grain terminal at Roseisle still remain. Thurso excepted, this was the last HR branch to survive. *P. Wylie*

The Muir of Ord–Fortrose branch, on the Black Isle, was 13½ miles long. Opened in February 1894, it was originally intended to run a little further, to Rosemarkie. The branch closed to passengers in October 1951 and to freight in June 1960. The station at Fortrose has been demolished, the site being now occupied by housing, but due to the flat and fertile nature of the Black Isle much of the branch has been returned to agriculture.

Elsewhere on the Black Isle a light railway was proposed from near Dingwall to Cromarty. More than 6 miles of track had been laid in the vicinity of Cromarty, and engineering works completed for a further 2 miles, by the time work was suspended upon the outbreak of World War 1 in 1914. After the war a Government committee deemed it inadvisable to build any new railways in the area, and the unfinished line was left to become derelict. The track was finally lifted in 1920, although a few traces remain today.

The line to the Kyle of Lochalsh could have run through Strathpeffer, but thanks to a difficult landowner, who wanted the line in a tunnel to reduce its impact on his grounds, the line had to be diverted to the north; a 2½-mile branch was thus built to the spa town, where a railway hotel was also opened. The

'Strathpeffer Spa Express', which ran on the branch until 1915, is covered in *Lost Lines: Scotland*. The branch closed to passengers in 1946 and to freight in 1951. The former trackbed of the branch, the ex-HR station and hotel all remain at Strathpeffer, and plans to reopen the branch have been put forward.

The scenic 7¾-mile branch from Dornoch to The Mound opened in June 1902, as a light railway. Although remaining independent until the Grouping

Below Fortrose station yard on 14 August 1959, with ex-CR 0-6-0 No 57594 taking water. The station house remains, but all other parts of the station have been demolished. By contrast Redcastle station survives and has been restored. *D. Capper*

in 1923, it was worked until that time by the HR. Holiday traffic to the sandy beaches and golf courses was significant, and the HR provided a hotel at Dornoch. For a brief period a through sleeping car to and from London was provided. The branch closed to all traffic in June 1960. Proposals in the 1980s to reopen it as part of a shorter main-line route to Wick, in conjunction with the new A9 road bridge being built across Dornoch Firth, came to naught.

And so we end this chapter with the last line to be opened and the most northerly standard-gauge lost passenger line in Britain. The Wick & Lybster Light Railway opened in July 1903 and was worked by the HR. It also had the distinction of being the most northerly light railway in the British Isles. Lybster was once the third-most-important herring port in Scotland, and this was the main reason for the construction of the 13¾-mile line. Three halts were added by the LMS, but the line closed as a World War 2 economy measure in April 1944. It never reopened for regular traffic and was officially closed in February 1951.

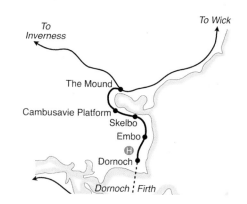

Right Timetable showing limited service between The Mound and Dornoch, July 1955.

Table 43												

THE MOUND and DORNOCH

	Miles		Week Days only						Miles		Week Days only	
			am	pm							am pm	
The Mound		dep	1155						Dornoch	dep	1025	1 0
Cambusavie Platform	1¼		12N4	2 5					Embo	2¼	1033	1 8
Skelbo	3¼		12N4	2N14					Skelbo	4	1045	1 20
Embo	5¼		1217	2 27					Cambusavie Platform	6¼	11N0	1N35
Dornoch	7¼	arr	1226	2 36					The Mound	7¼	arr 1111	1 46
			1238	2 48								

N Trains stop at Cambusavie on notice at Mound or Skelbo or when passengers on platform to be taken up

Below Pictured on 28 July 1913, HR 0-4-4T No 25 *Strathpeffer* has just arrived at the substantial station in the small spa town after which it was named. The refined Victorian charm of the spa resulted in the growth of tourism; shuttle services ran to Dingwall, there was an express service to Aviemore, and for a time a through coach to London was provided. *Ian Allan Library*

Top One of the last two ex-HR locomotives to survive, 0-4-4T No 55051 stands at Dornoch station on 4 September 1950 with a train for The Mound. The locomotives used on this branch were required to have a low axle weight, reflecting the fact that the line had been constructed as a light railway. The former station at building at Dornoch survives as a café. *B. Catterick*

Middle Ex-HR 0-4-4T No 55053 crosses the roadway at The Mound with a mixed train in July 1945. All crossings on the branch were unmanned and had to be operated by the guard on the train, with the result that journey times were slow. The Mound was named after Thomas Telford's road embankment. Today the station is closed, but disused platforms can still be found here. *Ian Allan Library*

Bottom End of the line. Some 742¾ miles by rail from Euston was Lybster station, terminus of the light railway from Wick – and looking deserted in this pre-World War 2 view. Extra passengers used the line in the 1920s and '30s, when, following Wick's decision to prohibit the sale of alcohol, drinkers travelled to bars along the route. The station building seen here is now used by the Lybster golf club, and an eroded concrete platform edge is still visible. The station building at Thrumster also survives. *Ian Allan Library*

23

Back on track.

Scotland has a number of lost lines that have been restored to use. The Strathspey Railway from Aviemore to Broomhill, in Inverness-shire, has plans to reach Grantown-on-Spey, the Bo'ness & Kinneil Railway, in West Lothian, has historic railway stock and buildings from throughout Scotland, while the Caledonian Railway at Brechin in Aberdeenshire, with its classic branch-line atmosphere, and the Keith & Dufftown Railway in Banffshire, with its heritage DMUs, are significant heritage lines that have come back to life.

The Royal Deeside line, at Crathes in Aberdeenshire, and the Scottish Industrial Railway Centre, at Dunaskin in Ayrshire, both provide shorter sections of standard-gauge line. The Waverley Route Heritage Association in the Borders has stock at Whitrope and is running trains on the line south toward Riccarton Junction.

The Leadhills & Wanlockhead Railway in Lanarkshire, the Grampian Transport Museum, with the adjoining Alford Valley Railway in Aberdeenshire, and the Almond Valley Heritage Trust in West Lothian all provide working narrow-gauge lines. The Glasgow Riverside Museum of Transport & Travel, the Prestongrange Industrial Heritage Museum in East Lothian and Summerlee Heritage Park in Lanarkshire all have Scottish-related railway stock and other fascinating railway

Left Keith Town station on 19 June 1967, with a Cravens DMU forming the 15.45 Cairnie Junction–Elgin. Closed to passengers in 1968, the wooden station buildings were later demolished, but in 2001 the Keith–Dufftown line was reopened as the 'Whisky Line' – Britain's most northerly heritage railway – and the buildings seen here have been replaced. *J. Boyes*

Above The original stone-built station at Brechin. Constructed by the Aberdeen Railway in 1849, it was later extended by the CR, a new building being added at a right-angle to the original. Following a period of closure the Brechin–Bridge of Dun line was reopened by the Caledonian Railway (Brechin) as a heritage passenger line in 1993 (the year this photograph was taken), whereupon the station's future was assured. *Author*

Above The reopened line at Alloa in July 2011, the new station being located beyond the bridge. The author's earlier volume, *Lost Lines: Scotland*, includes a photograph taken from the exact same vantage-point in June 1993, at which time the tracks here were heavily overgrown. After a period of closure Stirling–Alloa passenger services were restored in 2008, coinciding with a resumption of freight traffic to Kincardine. *John Roddis*

items. A number of closed stations have been preserved by their private owners.

Scotland's national rail network has expanded since the closures of the 1960s; there have been around 70 new or reopened stations on existing and reopened lines. The Edinburgh–Bathgate passenger service was revived in 1986, after a 30-year absence, and proved a great success. In 1992 Edinburgh's suburban services were restored to Newcraighall, and even the Edinburgh trams are making a return. The Larkhill line reopened in 2005, extending the Argyle line that witnessed the first major Scottish reopening, through central Glasgow, in 1979.

The railway reopened from Stirling to Alloa (and for freight to Kincardine) in 2008, and this has been a huge success. Services on the 15-mile Bathgate–Airdrie line commenced in 2010. This was the longest line to be (re)opened in Scotland since the opening of the Ballachulish branch in 1903. In 2012 work began on reopening the 35-mile northern part of the

former Waverley route, to Galashiels and Tweedbank in the Borders. The closure of the Waverley route in 1969 was possibly the most shameful act perpetrated in relation to the country's rail network.

The railways in Scotland are back on track. Yet the future is always uncertain, so why not also get back on track and visit Scotland's railways before too long? In the words of a CR poster, 'The Countryside Calls to you'.

Left Preserved CR McIntosh Class 812 0-6-0 No 828 waits to shunt stock at Boat of Garten station in 1993. Closed in 1969, the station was reopened in 1978 as part of the Strathspey Railway. Whether on a reopened heritage line or an existing part of the national network, some of the best scenic train rides in the world are to be found in Scotland. *G. Lumsden*

Right Hauled by a 1935 Kilmarnock-built Barclay 0-6-0T, *Braeriach*, a train departs from Bo'ness (Borrowstounness) station, on the Bo'ness & Kinneil Railway, in June 2011; the headboard celebrates 50 years of the Scottish Railway Preservation Society. On loan from the Strathspey Railway, the locomotive once ran on the Wemyss Coal Co railway and had been salvaged from a scrapyard in Fife. Partially visible on the right is preserved Class 27 diesel No 27 001. *Author*

Left Back on track in Scotland. South African Railways Class 15F 4-8-2 No 3007, built by the North British Locomotive Co in 1945, has returned home, having been donated by South African Railways to the Riverside Transport Museum in Glasgow. This close-up view of the four-coupled driving wheels and motion was recorded in October 2011. *Author's collection*